CAMBRIDGE PRIMARY
Science

Learner's Book

5

...ey and Jon Board

CAMBRIDGE
UNIVERSITY PRESS

CAMBRIDGE
UNIVERSITY PRESS

University Printing House, Cambridge CB2 8BS, United Kingdom

One Liberty Plaza, 20th Floor, New York, NY 10006, USA

477 Williamstown Road, Port Melbourne, VIC 3207, Australia

314–321, 3rd Floor, Plot 3, Splendor Forum, Jasola District Centre, New Delhi – 110025, India

79 Anson Road, #06–04/06, Singapore 079906

Cambridge University Press is part of the University of Cambridge.

It furthers the University's mission by disseminating knowledge in the pursuit of education, learning and research at the highest international levels of excellence.

www.cambridge.org
Information on this title: education.cambridge.org/9781107663046

First published 2014

20

Printed in Italy by Rotolito S.p.A.

A catalogue record for this publication is available from the British Library

ISBN 978-1-107-66304-6 Paperback

Cover artwork: Bill Bolton

....

NOTICE TO TEACHERS
Reference to Activities contained in these resources are provided 'as is' and information provided is on the understanding that teachers and technicians shall undertake a thorough and appropriate risk assessment before undertaking any of the Activities listed. Cambridge University Press makes no warranties, representations or claims of any kind concerning the Activities. To the extent permitted by law, Cambridge University Press will not be liable for any loss, injury, claim, liability or damage of any kind resulting from the use of the Activities.

Introduction

The *Cambridge Primary Science* series has been developed to match the Cambridge International Examinations Primary Science curriculum framework. It is a fun, flexible and easy to use course that gives both learners and teachers the support they need. In keeping with the aims of the curriculum itself, it encourages learners to be actively engaged with the content, and develop enquiry skills as well as subject knowledge.

This Learner's Book for Stage 5 covers all the content from Stage 5 of the curriculum framework. The topics are covered in the order in which they are presented in the curriculum for easy navigation, but can be taught in any order that is appropriate to you.

Throughout the book you will find ideas for practical activities, which will help learners to develop their Scientific Enquiry skills as well as introduce them to the thrill of scientific discovery.

The 'Talk about it!' question in each topic can be used as a starting point for classroom discussion, encouraging learners to use the scientific vocabulary and develop their understanding.

'Check your progress' questions at the end of each unit can be used to assess learners' understanding. Learners who will be taking the Cambridge Primary Progression test for Stage 5 will find these questions useful preparation.

We strongly advise you to use the Teacher's Resource for Stage 5, ISBN 978-1-107-67673-2, alongside this book. This resource contains extensive guidance on all the topics, ideas for classroom activities, and guidance notes on all the activities presented in this Learners' Book. You will also find a large collection of worksheets, and answers to all the questions from the Stage 5 products.

Also available is the Activity Book for Stage 5, ISBN 978-1-107-65897-4. This book offers a variety of exercises to help learners consolidate understanding, practise vocabulary, apply knowledge to new situations and develop enquiry skills. Learners can complete the exercises in class or be given them as homework.

We hope you enjoy using this series.

With best wishes,
the Cambridge Primary Science team.

Contents

Introduction   3

1 Investigating plant growth

1.1 Seeds   6
1.2 How seeds grow   8
1.3 Investigating germination   10
1.4 What do plants need to grow?   12
1.5 Plants and light   14
Check your progress   16

2 The life cycle of flowering plants

2.1 Why plants have flowers   18
2.2 How seeds are spread   20
2.3 Other ways seeds are spread   22
2.4 The parts of a flower   24
2.5 Pollination   26
2.6 Investigating pollination   28
2.7 Plant life cycles   30
Check your progress   32

3 States of matter

3.1 Evaporation   34
3.2 Why evaporation is useful   36
3.3 Investigating evaporation   38
3.4 Investigating evaporation from a solution   40
3.5 Condensation   42
3.6 The water cycle   44
3.7 Boiling   46
3.8 Melting   48
3.9 Who invented the temperature scale?   50
Check your progress   52

4 **The way we see things**

4.1	Light travels from a source	54
4.2	Mirrors	56
4.3	Seeing behind you	58
4.4	Which surfaces reflect light the best?	60
4.5	Light changes direction	62
	Check your progress	64

5 **Shadows**

5.1	Light travels in straight lines	66
5.2	Which materials let light through?	68
5.3	Silhouettes and shadow puppets	70
5.4	What affects the size of a shadow?	72
5.5	Investigating shadow lengths	74
5.6	Measuring light intensity	76
5.7	How scientists measured and understood light	78
	Check your progress	80

6 **Earth's movements**

6.1	The Sun, the Earth and the Moon	82
6.2	Does the Sun move?	84
6.3	The Earth rotates on its axis	86
6.4	Sunrise and sunset	88
6.5	The Earth revolves around the Sun	90
6.6	Exploring the solar system	92
6.7	Exploring the stars	94
	Check your progress	96

Reference	98
Glossary and index	105
Acknowledgements	110

1 Investigating plant growth

1.1 Seeds

Words to learn
seed   embryo
seed coat

Seeds and fruits

Have you ever swallowed a **seed** when you were eating an apple or an orange? We find seeds inside fruits. Fruits and seeds can be different sizes and shapes.

This apple has been cut in half to show the seeds.

An avocado pear has one large seed.

Bean seeds are found inside a pod.

A poppy's fruit contains the seeds.

What's inside a seed?

Are seeds alive? Seeds might look dead, but they are not. Seeds grow into new plants. There is a tiny plant inside the seed that starts to grow when it has all the things that it needs. The tiny plant inside the seed is called an **embryo**. The seed also has a food store.

Here is a bean seed with its parts labelled.

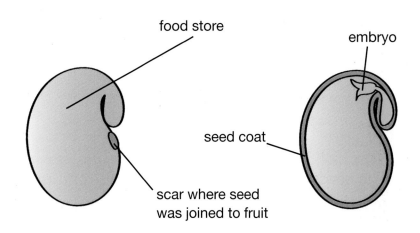

Activity 1.1

Draw and label a seed

Look carefully at the seed with the hand lens.

Find the **seed coat** and the scar where the seed was joined to the fruit.

Make a neat drawing of the outside of the seed. Label your drawing.

Use your fingernails to pull off the outer covering of the seed.

Pull the two halves of the seed apart.

Find the embryo inside the seed.

Find the seed's food store.

Draw and label the inside parts of the seed.

Questions

1 Why does the seed need a food store?

2 Why does the seed need a seed coat?

3 What do you think the seed needs to make it start to grow?

Talk about it!
What is the biggest seed in the world?

What you have learnt

- Seeds are found in fruits.
- The embryo inside a seed grows into a new plant.
- Seeds are covered by a seed coat.
- Seeds contain a food store.

1.2 How seeds grow

Words to learn
germination   shrivels
absorbs
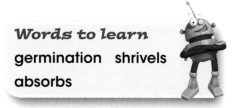

Germination

If a seed is given the right conditions, and the embryo is alive, it will grow.
When a seed starts to grow, we say it germinates. This process is called
germination. The seed uses its food store to give it the energy to grow.
The seed **shrivels** and becomes small after germination. Here are the stages in
germination of a bean seed.

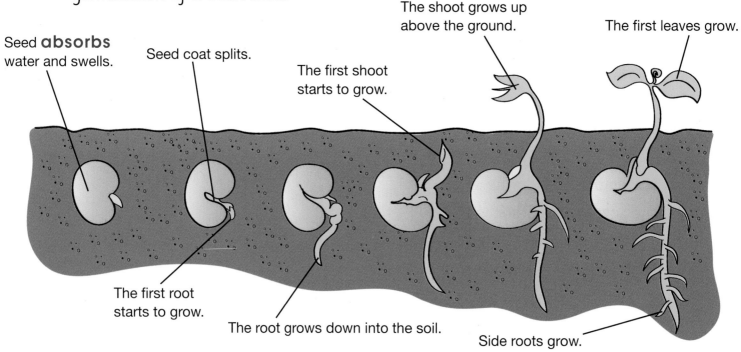

Seed **absorbs** water and swells.

Seed coat splits.

The first shoot starts to grow.

The shoot grows up above the ground.

The first leaves grow.

The first root starts to grow.

The root grows down into the soil.

Side roots grow.

A lotus plant growing in water.

Seeds can live without germinating for
years until the conditions become suitable.
The oldest seed known to germinate was
a 1300-year-old lotus seed found at the
bottom of a lake in China.

Activity 1.2

Observe a seed

Soak the bean seed in water overnight. Predict how the seed will change overnight.

Observe the seed the next day and write down any changes that you see.

How did the seed change overnight? Was your prediction correct? Explain why the changes happen. Where do you think the water entered the seed? Give a reason for your answer.

Questions

1 Why do seeds need to absorb water?

2 **a** Which part of the new bean plant grows first?

 b Suggest a reason why this part grows downwards.

3 In which direction does the first shoot grow and why?

4 Why do you think the new leaves start to grow above the ground?

5 Why do you think the seed shrivels and becomes small after germination?

Talk about it!
Can new plants only grow from seeds?

What you have learnt

- Seeds start to germinate if the conditions are right and the embryo is alive.
- The food store gives seeds the energy they need for germination.
- Seeds absorb water to start germination.
- The new root grows downwards first, followed by the new shoot which grows upwards.

1.3 Investigating germination

What do germinating seeds need?

Seeds germinate when they have the right conditions.

Can seeds germinate without water or light?

Will seeds germinate if it is very hot or very cold?

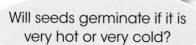

Activity 1.3a

Do seeds need air to germinate?

You will need:
20 small seeds · four paper towels · some water
two saucers · two small plastic bags · two bag ties
a drinking straw

Place 10 seeds on a moist paper towel on each saucer.

Cover both saucers with moist paper towels. Place one saucer in each bag.

Use the straw to suck all the air out of one bag. Quickly close it with a bag tie.

Close the other bag, leaving air inside it.

Leave both bags in a warm place for two days, then remove the seeds from the bags and observe them.

Which seeds germinated?

Suggest a reason for this.

Activity 1.3b

Investigate conditions needed for germination

Place five seeds against
the glass in each jar.
Moisten the soil in two jars.

moist soil or sawdust

dry soil or sawdust

seed

Place one jar of dry soil and one jar of moist soil in a warm place.

Place one jar of dry soil and one jar of moist soil in a cold place.

Check the moist soil every day to make sure it does not dry out.

Observe the seeds every two days for eight days.

Draw a table to record your observations.

Questions

1 How can you make sure that this is a fair test?

2 **a** What differences did you observe between the jars?

   b Suggest reason for these differences.

   c Why would your results be better if you used 40 seeds instead of 20?

3 Does the investigation show whether seeds need air for germination? Explain your answer.

4 Write a conclusion about the best conditions for seed germination.

5 **a** Do you think seeds need light for germination? Make a prediction.

   b Plan an investigation to test your prediction.

Talk about it!

Why do most seeds germinate in spring?

What you have learnt

🌀 Seeds germinate when they have right conditions.

🌀 Seeds need water, warmth and air to germinate.

🌀 Seeds do not need light to germinate.

1.4 What do plants need to grow?

Plants need certain things from the environment
to make them grow. We call these things **factors**.
Without these factors, plants will not grow well, or they might even die.
Look at these pictures. Which plant is healthy and growing well?

Plants need water, warmth, light and air

Plants need water so that they can have strong stems and firm
leaves. They also use water to transport substances such as
food to all parts of the plant.

Most plants grow best when they get warmth.
Most grow better if it is not too hot or too cold.

Plants make their own food. They need light energy
for this. A plant that does not get light energy
grows long, thin stems, becomes weak and dies.

Plants are living things. Living things need air.
Plants without air will die.

Plants need light
energy to grow.

Light energy is a factor that helps plants to grow.
Plants need the energy in sunlight to make food in their
leaves. Plants always grow towards the source of light energy.

Activity 1.4

Draw a bar chart of plant growth

Ashok and his friends grew some plants in pots.

Ashok put his plant in a sunny place and watered it twice a week.

Marco put his plant in a shady place and watered it twice a week.

Leo put his plant in sunny place but forgot to water it.

Tariq kept his plant under bed and watered it twice a week.

After two weeks they measured how much their plants had grown.

Name	How the plants looked	Growth of plants in cm
Ashok	green and healthy	25
Marco	lighter green and quite healthy	18
Leo	dry and brown	6
Tariq	thin and weak	14

Draw a bar chart of the results.

Questions

1 Whose plant grew the best?

2 Whose plant grew the worst?

3 Why did Leo's plant look dry and brown?

4 Why was Marco's plant smaller than Ashok's?

5 Explain why Tariq's plant was thin and weak.

6 a Predict the height of a plant placed in a greenhouse and watered. Explain your prediction.

   b Draw another bar on your chart to show your prediction.

Talk about it!

Do plants need soil for growth?

What you have learnt

- Plants need factors from the environment to make them grow.
- The factors plants need are light energy, air, water and warmth.

1.5 Plants and light

Activity 1.5

Investigating the effect of light on plant growth

Measure and record the height of the two plants.

Water both plants with the same amount of water.

Look at the pictures to see what to do.

Predict how well you think the two plants will grow. Write down your prediction.

Plant A

Plant B

Observe the plants every four days for three weeks. Water both plants with the same amount of water each time you observe them.

Draw a table to record the height and appearance each time you observe them.

	Date:		Date:		Date:		Date:		Date:	
	Plant A	Plant B	Plant A	Plant B	Plant A	Plant B	Plant A	Plant B	Plant A	Plant B
Height in cm										
Number of leaves										
Colour of stem and leaves										
General appearance										

Decide what type of graph is best to show your results.

Draw a graph of the plants' growth in height.

Draw the plants at the end of the investigation. Label your drawings.

Questions

1. a Which plant grew the best?

    b Do your results support your prediction?

    c Name two ways in which you measured plant growth.

    d How else could you tell which plant grew better?

2. a Why did you keep one plant in the dark?

    b Which factor or factors caused the changes you observed?

    c Is this investigation a fair test? Explain why or why not.

3. a Write a conclusion for the investigation.

    b Do you think you have enough data to form a conclusion? Say why or why not.

    c Suggest a way to improve your results without doing the investigation again.

4. If you repeated the investigation with a different type of plant, would you get the same results? Say why or why not.

Challenge

Design a fair test to show that plants need air to make them grow.

What you have learnt

🌀 Plants need light energy to grow well.

🌀 Plants need light energy to make food in their leaves.

Talk about it!

Why do some plants that live in very shady places grow big?

Check your progress

1 Copy the two columns of words.

Match the words in column A with their meanings in column B.

Column A

1	seed
2	embryo
3	seed coat
4	germinate
5	environment

Column B

A	the outer cover that protects the seed
B	when a seed start to grow
C	everything around us
D	part of a plant that can grow into a new plant
E	part of a seed that grows into a new plant

2 Copy and complete these sentences.
Use the words in the box to help you.

> food store   factor   air   shoot   root   swells   warmth   up
>
> down   absorbs

When a seed starts to germinate it _____ water and _____ .
The seed gets energy from its _____ .
The _____ is the first part of the new plant that starts to grow.
It grows _____ . The _____ grows next.
It grows _____ .
Seeds need water, _____ and _____ to germinate.
Light is a _____ that plants need so that they can grow.

3 Here is a picture of a germinating seed. Write down the names of parts 1 to 4.

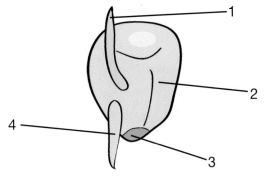

4 Dembe's class germinated seeds under different conditions. These are their results.

Conditions	Number of seeds germinated
warm, light	10
warm, dark	15
cold, light	5
cold, dark	7

a Which conditions are best for germination?

b Do seeds need light for germination? Use the results to explain your answer.

c Did the seeds get water or not? How do you know this?

d Dembe must draw a graph of the results. What type of graph should he draw and why?

5 Each plant in the picture is missing one of the factors it needs for growth.

a Identify the missing factor for each plant.

b Name one other factor that plants need for growth.

c Explain why the factor missing in A is important for plant growth.

A   B

2.1 Why plants have flowers

Words to learn
scent   wither
reproduce

Many plants have flowers. There are many different kinds of flowers.

Seeds form inside fruits. But where do fruits come from?

Why do plants have flowers? Is it to smell nice?

What job do flowers do?

No matter what the size, colour or **scent**, all flowers do the same important job. Can you think what it is?

Some flowers are big.

Some flowers are small.

Some flowers are colourful.

Some flowers are not brightly coloured.

Some flowers have scent. Others do not have scent.

When a plant produces flowers, the flowers usually last only a few days. Then they **wither** and fall off the plant. However, part of the flower stays behind on the plant. This part becomes the fruit. The seeds form inside the fruit. The seeds grow into new plants. The new plants grow and produce flowers to form new fruits and seeds. So flowers help the plant **reproduce** to form new plants.

Activity 2.1

Collect flowers

You will need:
different flowers

Collect a range of different flowers.
Group the flowers according to their size, colour and scent.
How many groups can you make?
Draw pictures of the flowers.
Try to name the flowers.

Questions

1 Copy and complete these sentences.
    _____ germinate and grow into new _____ .
    The plants form _____ that become fruits. The fruits
    contain _____ .
2 Why don't we usually find flowers and fruits
    on a peach tree at the same time?

Talk about it!
Which plants do not
have flowers?

What you have learnt

- Most plants have flowers, but not all do.
- Flowers can be big or small, colourful or non-coloured, scented or unscented.
- Flowers form fruits.
- Flowers help plants to reproduce.

2.2 How seeds are spread

A fruit has two jobs:

- to protect the seeds inside
- to help spread the seeds.

Have you ever found seeds stuck in your socks? Plants need to scatter their seeds away from themselves. We call this **seed dispersal**.

Why seeds must be dispersed

Why do you think seeds must be dispersed? What would happen if all the seeds grew next to their parent plant? What is happening to these seedlings?

Seedlings need room to grow. They also need light and water. Seedlings cannot grow to be healthy plants if they all have to share water and light in a small area. Plants disperse their seeds in different ways.

The pictures show how some plants disperse their seeds. Talk about how each seed is dispersed.

Some seeds are dispersed by animals

Animals can spread seeds. Birds, monkeys and even elephants eat colourful, juicy fruits. The seeds pass through the animal's body and are dispersed in the animal's droppings. This may be far away from where the animal ate the fruit.

Birds spread the seeds of berries and other fruits in their droppings.

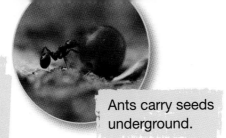
Ants carry seeds underground.

Seeds can be carried a long way from the parent plant before they fall off, or the animal scratches them off.

Some seeds have spines and hooks. These stick onto the fur of animals, or the clothes of people. Mice, ants and squirrels carry seeds away from the parent plant and bury them to eat later. If the animal does not eat the seeds, the seeds will germinate in the soil.

Activity 2.2

Researching seed dispersal

Do some research to find out more about how seeds are dispersed by animals. You can find information in books or from the internet. Make a poster with drawings or pictures to show your findings.

You will need:
access to the internet and/or reference books about plants

Questions

1 Which seeds would grow better: those in a tomato left on the plant or those in a tomato eaten by a bird? Say why.

2 Do you think peach seeds can be dispersed by animals? Say why or why not.

3 Make a drawing of a seed you think would be dispersed in an animal's fur.

Talk about it!
How is the seed of an avocado pear dispersed?

What you have learnt

- A fruit protects the seeds inside it and helps to spread the seeds.
- Seeds must be dispersed so they have enough space, water and light to grow into new plants.
- Seeds can be dispersed in different ways.
- Animals disperse seeds in their droppings, by carrying seeds on their fur and by burying them.

2.3 Other ways seeds are spread

Words to learn
spongy   explode

Can seeds be dispersed by wind?

Have you ever blown away the seeds of dandelion?
Seeds that are dispersed by wind are light and dry.

Dandelions have parachute of hairs to help them float in the air. Other seeds have thin papery 'wings' to help them blow away easily.

The fruits of the chandelier plant dry out and break off. As the wind blows them along, the seeds fall out.

The poppy fruit forms a 'pepper pot' with holes in it. When the wind blows, the seeds are shaken out and blown away.

The seed of the maple tree has wings that allow the wind to lift and spin it like helicopter rotor blades and carry it away.

Can seeds be dispersed by water?

A few seeds are dispersed by water. These seeds must float. They have a **spongy** covering that helps them float. The coconut is dispersed by water.

Mangroves are trees that grow in salty water in warm, wet regions. Their seeds, called 'sea pencils', float upright in the sea until they are washed onto land.

Some seeds explode

Some fruits disperse their seeds by themselves.
They **explode** and shoot out their seeds.

Bean pods dry out and explode in hot weather when the seeds are ripe.

Activity 2.3

How are seeds dispersed?

Collect at least five different kinds of seeds.
Observe each seed carefully with a hand lens.
Try to identify which plant each seed comes from.
Make a drawing of each seed. Label your drawings.
Say how you think the seed is dispersed and why.

You will need:
different kinds of seeds • a hand lens

Questions

1 How does a spongy seed coat help a water lily to disperse its seeds?
2 Why are bean pods usually picked before the weather gets hot and dry?
3 How do think the bush willow seed is dispersed? Give a reason for your answer.

Bush willow seed.

Talk about it!
Which type of seed dispersal spreads the seeds furthest from the parent plant?

What you have learnt

🌀 Seeds dispersed by wind are light and dry to help them blow away easily.
🌀 Seeds dispersed by water float until they are washed up on land.
🌀 Some seed pods explode to disperse their seeds.

2.4 The parts of a flower

Words to learn

sepals	stamen
carpel	ovary
pollen	anther
stigma	

Activity 2.4a

You will need:
a flower • a hand lens

Investigating the parts of a flower

Look at the flower. What colour is it?

Count the coloured parts. What are they called? Are these parts separate or joined?

Find the little green parts that look like leaves at the base of the flower. How many are there?

Look inside the flower. This is where you find the male parts and female parts. Count the little thin stalks. How many stalks have yellow or brown tips? Touch their tips gently. What do you notice on your fingers?

Look for a single stalk in the centre of the flower that looks different. Touch the tip. How does it feel?

Flowers have these main parts. These parts are arranged in rings, one inside the other.

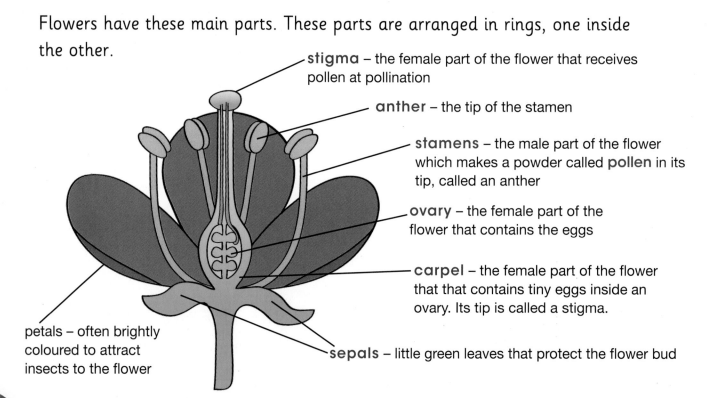

stigma – the female part of the flower that receives pollen at pollination

anther – the tip of the stamen

stamens – the male part of the flower which makes a powder called **pollen** in its tip, called an anther

ovary – the female part of the flower that contains the eggs

carpel – the female part of the flower that that contains tiny eggs inside an ovary. Its tip is called a stigma.

sepals – little green leaves that protect the flower bud

petals – often brightly coloured to attract insects to the flower

Activity 2.4b

Observe and draw a flower

Draw the flower and label its parts.

Count and record the number of petals, sepals and stamens.

Can you see a pattern?

Carefully pull off the petals and sepals with the tweezers.

Use the hand lens to look at the stamens and the carpel.

Make a labelled drawing of a stamen.

Make a labelled drawing of the carpel.

Questions

1   Name the parts of a flower that:
    a make pollen
    b protect the flower bud
    c contain eggs
    d attract insects and birds.

2   Which part of the flower do you think makes scent?

3   Flower petals are different colours. Plan an investigation to find out which colour is most common.

This flower smells like rotting meat.

Talk about it!

Why are some flowers dark reddish brown with a scent like rotting meat?

What you have learnt

🌀 Flowers have four main parts: green sepals protect the flower bud, coloured petals attract insects, male stamens make pollen and the female carpel contains eggs.

2.5 Pollination

Have you noticed bees, butterflies and other insects on flowers? They are moving pollen from the stamen to the stigma of a flower. The process is called **pollination**. In pollination, the pollen moves the stamen to the stigma of the same kind of flower.

This bee is pollinating a flower.

There are two main ways that pollen is carried from the stamens to the stigma — by insects or by wind.

Pollination by insects

Flowers pollinated by insects usually have brightly coloured, scented petals. Some flowers also make **nectar**, a sweet liquid. Insects visit the flowers to feed on the nectar. They get covered in pollen and carry the pollen to the stigma of the same flower or another flower.

Pollination by wind

Flowers pollinated by wind are not brightly coloured and do not have petals or scent. Wind-pollinated flowers make lots of pollen. Pollen blows in the wind from the stamens to the stigmas of other flowers.

The wind blows the pollen from this grass flower to other flowers.

Activity 2.5

Which type of pollination?

You will need:
hand lens • paper • pencils

Look at different flowers in the school grounds, local community park, or in pictures. Draw pictures of the flowers and label their parts. Decide how each flower is pollinated and why.

Why must flowers be pollinated?

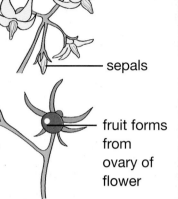

flower

sepals

Plants reproduce by making seeds. The pollen and eggs join to make seeds in a process called **fertilisation**.

Pollination brings pollen from the male stamen to the female carpel. This allows the eggs to be fertilised and seeds to form. Fertilisation happens in the flower's ovary. Fertilisation only happens if the pollen and the eggs are from the same kind of flower.

fruit forms from ovary of flower

After the egg is fertilised, the petals and stamens of the flower die. The ovary grows and becomes the fruit. Seeds are inside the fruit.

mature fruit

Questions

1   Why do flowers pollinated by insects have brightly coloured, scented petals and nectar?

2   **a** Why do flowers pollinated by wind have little colour, no petals or scent?
     b Why do flowers pollinated by wind produce lots of dry pollen?

3   How does pollination help the plant reproduce?

4   Explain how pollination is different to fertilisation.

Challenge

Find out how the pollen gets to the ovary of the flower.

Talk about it!

Why do insects see white flowers as purple?

What you have learnt

- Pollination brings pollen from the stamen to the stigma of a flower of the same kind.
- Flowers pollinated by insects have brightly coloured, scented petals and nectar.
- Flowers pollinated by wind have little colour, no petals or scent and lots of pollen.
- Fertilisation happens when the pollen and eggs join inside the ovary.
- The fertilised eggs become seeds and the ovary becomes the fruit.

2.6 Investigating pollination

Certain insects are attracted to certain types of flowers. For example, butterflies like to visit flowers that are big and have lots of nectar. Bees, beetles, wasps, ants and moths also pollinate flowers.

This flower has lots of nectar to attract the butterfly.

This flower attracts beetles.

This flower attracts bees.

Activity 2.6

Observing insect pollinators

You will need:
plants that have flowers • a watch

Find four different plants with flowers.

Look for flowers that are brightly coloured as well as some that do not have bright colours, such as grass flowers.

Observe the flowers. What size and colour are they? Do they have lots of pollen? Do they have nectar?

Predict how each flower is pollinated.

Observe which types of insects visit the flowers.

Count how many times the different insects visit the flowers in half an hour.

Record your observations in a table like this one.

Name of flower	Description of flower	Prediction of how flower is pollinated	Insects that visit the flower	Number of visits

Draw a bar chart of your findings.

Questions

1 Which flowers did insects visit the most often? Suggest a reason why.

2 Which insects visited the flowers most often?

3 Were your predictions about pollination correct?

4 **a** What pattern could you observe in the flowers visited by insects?

   b Suggest a reason for the pattern.

Most red flowers are not pollinated by insects, but by birds such as sunbirds and humming birds.

Challenge

Find out why most red flowers are pollinated by birds rather than insects.

Talk about it!

Moths pollinate flowers at night. What kinds of flowers do you think they pollinate?

What you have learnt

- Certain insects pollinate certain types of flowers.
- Bees, butterflies, beetles and wasps are some insects that pollinate flowers.

2.7 Plant life cycles

Words to learn

life cycle

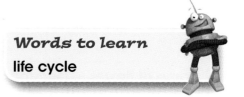

Think about all the changes in a plant's life, from a germinating seed until it develops into a grown plant and forms its own seeds. All these changes are called the plant's **life cycle**. Some plants die after they have made their seeds. Other plants flower and make seeds every year.

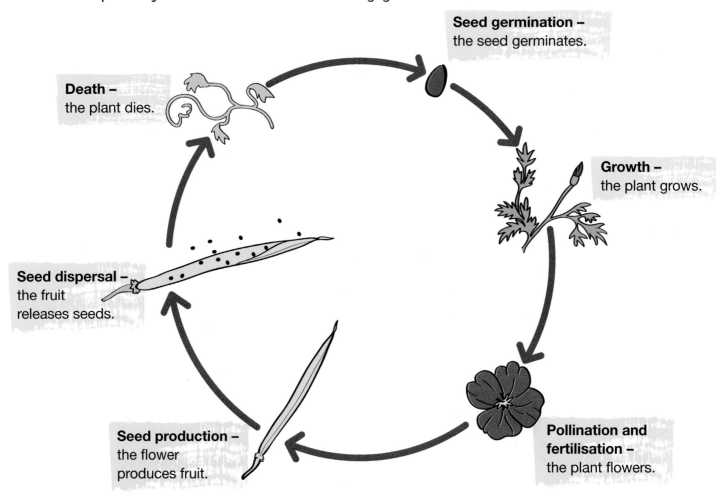

Seed germination – the seed germinates.

Growth – the plant grows.

Pollination and fertilisation – the plant flowers.

Seed production – the flower produces fruit.

Seed dispersal – the fruit releases seeds.

Death – the plant dies.

Questions

1   The diagram on the next page shows the stages of a tomato plant's life cycle. Match each of the processes to the stage of life cycle. Write your answers in a table.

Process	Stage of life cycle

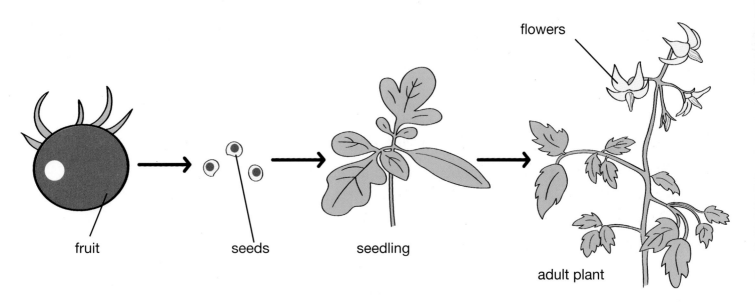

fruit   seeds   seedling   flowers   adult plant

2 These are the stages in the life cycle of a bean plant:

> flower   seedling   bean pod   adult plant   seed

The stages are in the wrong order. Put them in the right order and draw the life cycle of the bean plant with labels.

3 Why do we make life cycle drawings in a circle?

4 **a** Think of a plant that dies after it produces seeds.

    b Think of a plant that flowers and produces seeds every year.

Talk about it!

What are annual plants and perennial plants?

What you have learnt

- The plant starts life as a seed. It germinates and grows into a plant.
- The adult plant produces flowers, which are pollinated and fertilised to produce seeds in a fruit or seedpod.
- The seeds are dispersed and germinate to produce new plants.

2 Check your progress

1 **a** What is the process called when plants spread their seeds?

b Why is this process important?

c Explain **three** ways by which animals can spread their seeds.

d How are the seeds shown in the pictures spread? Give a reason for your answers.

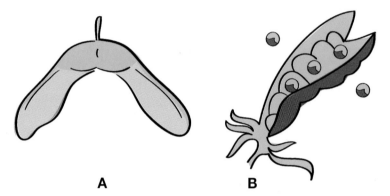

A   B

e Name **one** other way seeds can be dispersed and give an example.

2 **a** This drawing of a flower has some parts missing. Redraw the flower and add the missing parts from the list:

sepals
stamens
anther
ovary
stigma
eggs

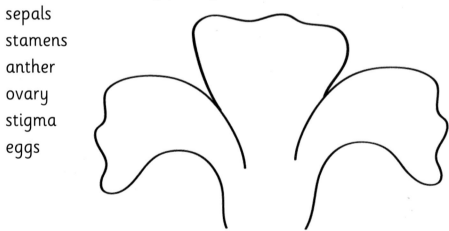

b Label all the parts of the drawing.

c Which part of the flower forms the seeds?

d Name the process by which the seeds are formed.

e Where does the process take place?

3 Look at the pictures of the two flowers.

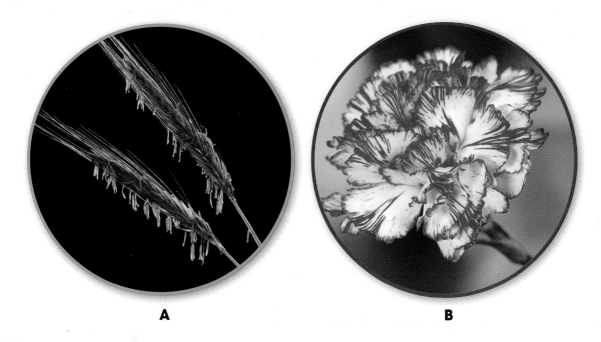

A   B

a Which flower is pollinated by insects? Give **two** reasons
   for your answer.
b Suggest an insect that could pollinate the flower.
c Which flower is pollinated by wind? Give **two** reasons for
   your answer.

4 Arrange these processes in the correct order and draw a life cycle
diagram for a plant.

fertilisation   germination   growth   seed dispersal
         pollination   seed production.

3 States of matter

3.1 Evaporation

Why does a puddle dry up
after the rain stops?
What happens to the water?

When water or other liquids
become warm enough,
they change into a gas.
Water changes into a gas
called **water vapour**. When liquids
change into gases we say they evaporate.

Evaporation happens because some particles in the
liquid gain heat **energy**. The heated particles start to
move faster and move further apart. Eventually the
heated particles move so far apart that they escape
from the surface of the liquid into the surrounding air.

Activity 3.1a

Where does the water go?

You will need:
a glass • water • sheet of construction paper

Dip your finger into the water.
Make a wet spot on the paper with your finger.
Leave the paper for a few minutes. Pick up the piece of paper. Is it wet or dry?
If it is dry, where did the water go?

Matter exists in three different states or phases. Matter can be solid, liquid or
gas. When water evaporates it changes from the liquid state to the gas state:

liquid + heat → gas

Activity 3.1b

You will need:
two identical glasses · water
a permanent marker · a measuring jug

Compare evaporation

Pour 100 ml of water into both glasses.

Mark the level of the water with a permanent marker.

Put one glass in a warm place.

Put the other glass in a cool place.

Leave the glasses for two days.

Mark the level of the water after two days.

Questions

1 Was the water level in the two glasses the same after two days?

2 Which glass had the least water and which glass had the most water after two days? Suggest reasons for this.

3 Why does washing dry quicker on a hot day?

Water can evaporate with the help of heat. Changes in temperature can increase or decrease how fast water evaporates.

Talk about it!
Why does wet paint smell but dry paint doesn't?

What you have learnt

- Evaporation happens when a liquid turns into a gas.
- When particles of water gain heat energy, they move faster and further apart and break free from the liquid's surface.
- Heat makes evaporation take place faster.

3.2 Why evaporation is useful

We use evaporation in many different ways.
Talk about how evaporation happens in each of the pictures and how it is useful.

drying your hair

grapes drying on a rack in the sun

using a tumble dryer

Evaporation cools things down

When we are hot, we sweat. As the fastest, hottest water particles in the sweat escape by evaporation, they take heat energy from our skin. Water needs energy to evaporate and change from a liquid to a gas. If this energy comes from the surface of your skin, your skin gets cooled.

When we sweat, our skin cools down.

Have you ever used hand sanitiser? The sanitiser evaporates off your hands making them feel cool.

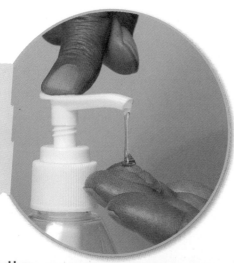

Liquids evaporate faster when the air is moving.

Sweating makes us cooler.

Activity 3.2

Get cool faster

Breathe onto the back of your hand. Does your breath feel warm or cool?

Blow onto the back of your hand. Does it feel warmer or cooler than your breath?

Now lick the back of your hand and then blow on it. Blow gently at first and then harder. What do you feel? Suggest a reason for your observation.

Questions

1 Explain two ways in which a hair dryer makes water evaporate from our hair.

2 a Think of **three** foods that are made by using evaporation.

   b Find more about how one of these foods is made.

3 Why do you think soil in the garden dries out more quickly on hot, windy days?

Dried fruit is made using evaporation.

What you have learnt

🍥 Evaporation helps us to dry things such as washing, our hair and food.

🍥 Liquids evaporate faster when the air is moving.

Talk about it!

Why is it better to stay fully clothed in a hot desert, even if you feel very hot?

3.3 Investigating evaporation

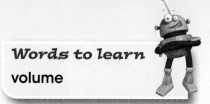
Activity 3.3a

How much water evaporates?

Pour 200 ml of water into each container. Put one container in a cool place, such as a cupboard and the other in a warm place, such as a sunny window ledge.

You will need:

two containers of the same size and shape
water • a measuring jug

warm place

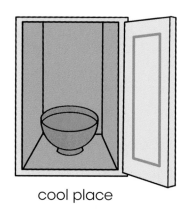

cool place

Measure the **volume** of water in each container every day for five days.
How will you do this?
Record your results in a table like this one.

Day	Volume of water in ml	
	Container in a warm place	**Container in a cool place**
1		

Questions

1 What pattern do you see in your results?

2 What kind of chart will you draw to show this pattern?

3 a What do your results tell you about evaporation?

   b How can you collect enough evidence to be sure your idea about evaporation is correct?

4 How can you change this investigation to find out how wind or moving air affects evaporation?

Activity 3.3b

Does the container affect evaporation?

You will need:
a measuring cup · containers with different size openings

Measure 100 ml of water and pour it into one container.
Repeat this with the other containers.
Place all the containers in the same place in a warm room. Leave them for three days.
Then measure the volume of water in each container.
Record your measurements in a table like this one.

jar   bowl   glass

baking tray

Container	Volume of water in ml

Questions

1 a What did you notice? Has the amount of water gone down in the containers?

b If so, in which containers has it gone down the most?

c What happened to the missing water?

2 a What was different about the containers?

b Explain how you think this affected your results.

3 Was your test a fair test? Say why or why not.

4 a What conclusion can you draw from these results?

b How can you be sure your conclusion is correct?

What you have learnt

🌀 More water evaporates in warm conditions than in cool conditions.

🌀 More evaporation takes place from larger surfaces of water than from smaller surfaces.

Talk about it!
Why do shallow reservoirs lose more water by evaporation than deep reservoirs?

3.4 Evaporation from a solution

Most of the salt we put on our food comes from sea water.

How can we get salt from sea water?

Solutions

Some materials can **dissolve** in water or other liquids. Materials that dissolve form **solutions**. Solutions always have two parts:

- The **solute** – the material that is dissolved.

- The **solvent** – the liquid in which the solute dissolves.

Salt works are used to extract salts from seawater using evaporation.

You cannot see the solute in a solution after it has dissolved. The particles of the solute move in between the solvent particles when they dissolve.

Activity 3.4a

Making a solution

Fill the glass beaker three-quarters full of water.
Put a teaspoon of the copper sulfate **crystals** into the jar and observe what happens.
Write down your observations.
What can you observe in the water around the copper sulfate?
Draw and label your observations.
Can you see the solid copper sulfate any more?
In this activity, which is the solute and which is the solvent?

You will need:
water • copper sulfate crystals
a glass beaker • a teaspoon

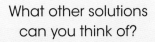

What other solutions can you think of?

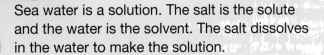

Sea water is a solution. The salt is the solute and the water is the solvent. The salt dissolves in the water to make the solution.

Activity 3.4b

Can you get the salt back?

Can you use your knowledge of evaporation to get solid salt from a salt solution?

> **You will need:**
> salt • water • a small container
> a measuring jug • a teaspoon

Make a salt solution from 5 ml of salt and 50 ml of water.

Predict what will happen when you evaporate a salt solution.

Give a reason for your prediction.

Think about how to set up your investigation.

Where should you set up the investigation?

How long must you leave it to get any results?

Make a labelled drawing to show what you used and what you did.

Make a labelled drawing to show the results of your investigation.

Questions

1 Was your prediction correct?
2 Suggest **two** ways in which you could obtain results faster.
3 Write a conclusion by completing this sentence.
   I found out that it was possible/impossible to separate a solid from a liquid by evaporation.

What you have learnt

- A solution is made up of a solute dissolved in a solvent.
- The particles of the solute move in between the solvent particles when they dissolve so you cannot see the solute in the solution.
- When a liquid evaporates from a solution, the solid solute is left behind.

Talk about it!
When you mix orange cordial with water, is it a solution or not? Why?

3.5 Condensation

Breathe onto a window pane
or a mirror. What do you observe?

You should see tiny drops of liquid on the mirror. What are the drops made of? Why do they form?

The air you breathe out is warm. It contains water vapour. When the warm air touches a cooler surface, like the mirror, it cools down. If the surface is cold enough, the water vapour gas changes to drops of liquid water. The process is called **condensation**. It is the **reverse** of evaporation.

Condensation happens because the particles of a gas lose energy when they get cooler. This makes them slow down and move closer together forming a liquid.

A drink can with condensation on the outside.

Activity 3.5a

Where does the water come from?

Look at the picture to see how to set up
your investigation.
Wipe both the glasses with a cloth.
Leave the glasses for 10 min and then observe them.
Make labelled drawings of your observations.

You will need:
two glasses · ice · water
a measuring jug · a cloth

Questions

1   Were either of the glasses wet on the outside at the
    start of the investigation? How did you make sure of this?

2   **a** Were either of the glasses wet on the outside at the end of the
    investigation? If so, which glasses?
    b Where did the water come from and why?

3   Condensation is the reverse of evaporation. Explain why this is so.

Activity 3.5b

Observing evaporation and condensation

You will need:
two glasses · plastic wrap and water
a measuring jug · a marker pen

Pour 100 ml of water into both glasses. Mark the water level on the outside of the glasses with the marker pen. Cover one glass tightly with a piece of plastic wrap. Leave both the glasses in warm place overnight and examine them the next day.

Questions

1 Is the amount of water in the glasses still the same?

2 What do you observe in the covered glass that is different to the open glass?

3 How did you make this a fair test?

4 Copy and complete these sentences using these words.

> water vapour   water droplets   heat   condensed   evaporated

The water in the open glass gained _____ and _____
to form _____ .
In the closed glass the water vapour cooled and _____
to form _____ on
the plastic wrap.

What you have learnt

- Condensation happens when a gas changes to a liquid.
- When gas particles cool down and lose energy they change into a liquid.
- Condensation is the opposite of evaporation.

Talk about it!
How could people use evaporation and condensation to clean drinking water?

3 States of matter   43

3.6 The water cycle

Water keeps going around and around in what we call the **water cycle**. In the water cycle, water moves from the land and sea to the air and back again.

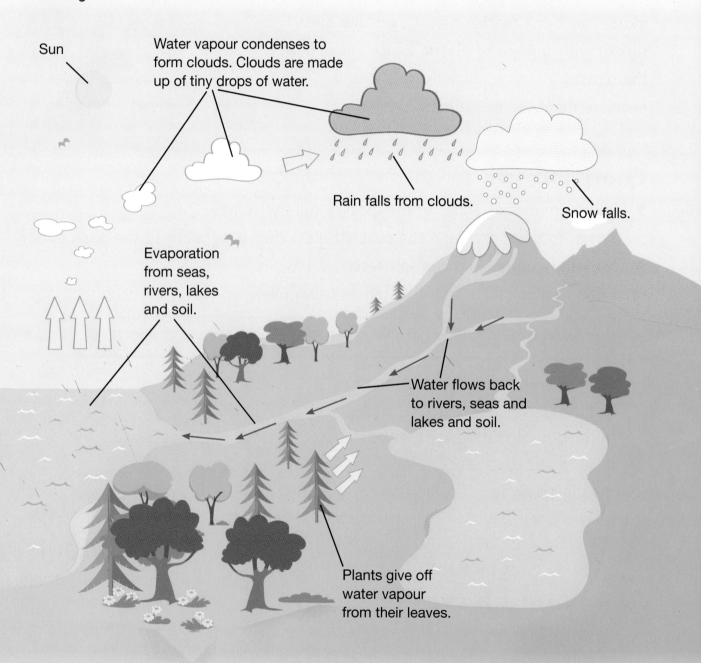

Sun

Water vapour condenses to form clouds. Clouds are made up of tiny drops of water.

Rain falls from clouds.

Snow falls.

Evaporation from seas, rivers, lakes and soil.

Water flows back to rivers, seas and lakes and soil.

Plants give off water vapour from their leaves.

The water cycle happens mainly because of evaporation and condensation. Freezing and melting also happen in the water cycle.

Questions

1 **a** Where does the heat come from that makes water evaporate from rivers, lakes and seas?

   b Where else in the water cycle does evaporation happen?

2 Where does the evaporated water go?

3 **a** What happens to water vapour when it condenses?

   b Where in the water cycle does this happen?

4 How does the evaporated water get back to Earth?

5 Where in the water cycle does:

   a freezing happen?

   b melting happen?

6 Why is the water cycle important to us?

7 Complete these sentences about the water cycle.
Use the words in the box to help you.

> water   vapour   condenses   evaporates

   a Water on the Earth's surface _____ and moves up into the air as water _____ .

   b The water vapour cools and _____ as it rises into the air.

   c Rain, snow and hail bring _____ back to the Earth's surface.

Talk about it!
Can the water cycle ever end?

What you have learnt

- The water cycle is the movement of water from the Earth's surface into the air and back again.
- In the water cycle, water evaporates from the Earth's surface, condenses to form clouds and falls back to Earth as rain.

3.7 Boiling

Words to learn

boil   steam

boiling point

Ouch! I've burnt my hand and I didn't even touch the pot.

It's so hot above the pot. Why?

Why did Harry burn his hand?

If we heat water enough it will **boil**.
We can show how boiling happens like this:

liquid + heat → gas

Activity3.7a

What happens when water boils?

Your teacher will boil some water.
Observe what happens as the water gets hotter.
Describe what happens to the water.
How does the boiling water look?
Hold your hand high above the boiling water. How does it feel?

You will need:
water · a beaker or pan · a hotplate or Bunsen burner

Safety

Boiling water can be dangerous. Both the water and the steam can burn you badly.

When a liquid boils it changes into a gas. The particles of the liquid gain heat and move much more quickly. Some of the heated particles move so far apart that they escape from the surface of the liquid and become a gas.

Water changes into **steam** when it boils. Steam is heated water vapour.

When a liquid gets hot enough to boil we say it has reached its **boiling point**. Different liquids have different boiling points. How hot is water's boiling point?

Activity 3.7b

Investigating the boiling point of water

You will need:
water • a beaker or pan • a hotplate or Bunsen burner • a thermometer • a watch

Your teacher will boil some water in a beaker or a pan.

He or she will measure the temperature of the water every two minutes until the water boils. Record your teacher's measurements in a table like this one.

Time in minutes	Water temperature in °C

Record the temperature of the water every two minutes for four minutes after the water has started boiling.

Safety Boiling water can be dangerous. Both the water and the steam can burn you badly.

Questions

1 **a** What pattern can you see in the results?

 b What sort of chart will you draw to show the results?

2 **a** At what temperature did the water boil?

 b Will water always boil at this temperature? How can you find out?

3 Did the temperature increase after the water started to boil? Why do you think this is so?

4 **a** What are the bubbles in the boiling water?

 b Why do you think they form ?

Challenge

Why does water not always boil at 100 °C?

Talk about it!

What is the difference between evaporation and boiling?

What you have learnt

- When water boils it changes from a liquid to a gas called steam.
- Particles of liquid water gain energy when they are heated and change into a gas.
- The boiling point of pure water is 100 °C.

3.8 Melting

Words to learn

melts   melting point

When a material **melts**, it changes from a solid to a liquid. We can show how melting happens like this:

solid + heat → liquid

When solids are heated, their particles gain energy and start to move more quickly and pull further apart. If the particles gain enough energy, they escape from the solid and change into a liquid.

The temperature at which a solid melts is called its **melting point**.
Different solids have different melting points.

What happens to the butter when it's heated?

As the solid ice melts, it changes to a liquid.

The filament in this light bulb is made of tungsten. Tungsten is a very hard metal. It has a melting point of 3380 °C.

Metals melt at very high temperatures.

Activity 3.8

Investigating the melting point of ice

Put the ice in the beaker.

Measure the temperature of the ice every minute
until it melts.

Carry on measuring the temperature in the beaker every minute
for another 10 minutes.

Record your measurements in a table like this one.

Time in minutes	Temperature of ice in °C

Questions

1 a What pattern can you see in the results?

   b What sort of chart will you draw to show the results?

2 a At what temperature did the ice melt?

   b Will water always melt at this temperature?
How can you find out?

   c How could you make the ice melt faster?

3 a Predict what the temperature of the melted ice will be 20 minutes
after it has melted. Explain your prediction.

   b Test your prediction. Were you correct?

4 The melting point of ice is 0°C. This is the same
temperature as the freezing point of water.
Why do think this is so?

What you have learnt

- Melting is when a solid changes into a liquid.
- Particles within a solid gain energy when they are
heated and change into a liquid.
- The melting point of ice is 0°C.

Talk about it!

How does putting salt
on frozen roads make
the roads less icy?

3.9 Who invented the temperature scale?

Does water always boil at 100°C? The answer is 'Yes' and 'No'.

Gabriel Daniel Fahrenheit 1686–1736

Fahrenheit invented the first thermometer but scientists could not agree on a temperature scale for the thermometer. Fahrenheit invented a new scale.
He decided that the coldest temperature he could make by mixing different substances was 0°. On Fahrenheit's temperature scale, water freezes into ice at 32° and boils at 212°. This scale is still used in some countries, including the USA.

Anders Celsius 1701–1744

Celsius was also interested in measuring temperature. He suggested a temperature scale from 0° to 100°, with water boiling at 0° and ice melting at 100°. Other scientists told him it was strange for hot things to have a lower temperature than cold things, so Celsius reversed his scale. He made 0° the temperature at which ice melts and 100° the temperature at which water boils. This is the scale that we use today. We measure the temperature in degrees Celsius (°C).

Lord Kelvin (William Thomson) 1824–1907

Kelvin and other scientists were researching the lowest temperature possible. Kelvin invented a temperature scale to measure things that are so cold that their particles do not move at all, and everything, including air, freezes solid. This temperature is 0° on Kelvin's scale. He called this temperature 'absolute zero'. It is the same temperature as −273°C. On the Kelvin scale, water freezes at 273° and boils at 373°.

You will need:
A3 paper • colouring pens • access to the internet

Which temperature scale?

Choose one of the three temperature scales on the opposite page.

Create a poster about the temperature scale and list some melting and boiling points of some everyday materials, such as water, butter, chocolate and any others you wish to include.

You will need to do some research about melting and boiling points using books or the internet.

You should also write about the history of the temperature scale and include it on your poster.

Questions

1 Why do you think scientists needed to invent a temperature scale, instead of just deciding if things were hot or cold?

2 a How did Celsius decide on his scale?
  b How did he later change it?

3 a Why did Kelvin invent the Kelvin scale?
  b What is 'absolute zero'?

4 a What similarity can you see in Kelvin's and Celsius' temperature scales?
  b How are the two scales different?

5 Which temperature scale do you think is easiest to use? Say why.

This thermometer measures temperature using both the Fahrenheit and Celsius scales.

What you have learnt

⦿ Different scientists have invented different temperature scales.

⦿ We mostly measure temperature in Celsius. On this scale, ice melts at 0°C and water boils at 100°C.

Talk about it!
The Celsius temperature scale is also sometimes called the centigrade scale. Why is this?

1 Write the word that describes each of the following processes:

   a a liquid changes into a gas

   b a gas changes into a liquid

   c a solid changes into a liquid

   d water changes into ice

   e heated water changes into steam.

2 Saria and Amira grew some plants for their classroom. Saria's plants needed to be watered everyday. Amira's plants did not.

My plants don't need as much water.

   a What process has made Saria's plants need water everyday?

   b Why do Amira's plants need less water?

   c Suggest **two** things Saria can do to make her plants need less water.

3 Luisa went into the bathroom after her sister had a bath.
It was full of mist and the mirror was covered in drops of liquid.

  a What was the mist made of?

  b What were the drops of liquid made of?

  c Name the process that made the drops of liquid form.

  d Why did the drops form?

4 Label the processes that take place at points A–D on the diagram of
the water cycle.

5 Look at these pictures.

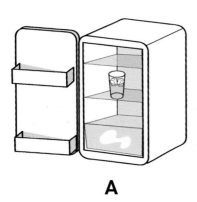

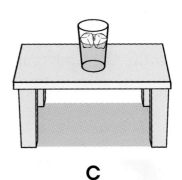

      A   **B**   **C**

  a Which ice cubes will melt the fastest? Why?

  b Will the ice cubes in A melt at a lower temperature than the ice
  cubes in B? Explain your answer.

  c What happens to ice when it melts?

4.1 Light travels from a source

Activity 4.1a

You will need:

a torch with cells · a dark cupboard

Investigating light from a torch

Switch on the torch. Observe the light. Does the light come from the torch or go into the torch?

Light sources

The torch you used in Activity 4.1a is a **light source**. Light travels from the torch in bands. A band of light is called a **beam** of light.

Our main source of light is the Sun. Light travels from the Sun in beams.

Identify the light sources in the pictures.

How we see things

Light travels from the light source to the **object**. The light bounces or **reflects** off the object into your eyes. This is how you see the object.

Activity 4.1b

Investigate how we see an object

Cut two holes in the lid of the box as shown in the picture. One hole must be big enough for your torch to fit through. The other hole must be big enough for you to see through. Place the small object (coin) on the bottom of the box and replace the lid on the box.

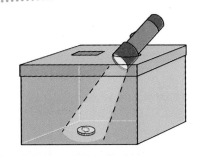

Cover the torch hole with your hand.
Predict whether you will be able to see the small object. Test your prediction.
Shine your torch through the torch hole.
Predict whether you will be able to see the small object now. Test your prediction.

Questions

1 Identify the source of light in the picture.
2 Explain, with a drawing, how the person can see the car. You can draw lines with arrows to show the direction in which the light travels.
3 Discuss how the person could see the car at night.

What you have learnt

🌀 Light travels from a light source.
🌀 Light reflects off objects into our eyes.

Talk about it!
Where is the best position for a lamp you use to read in the dark?

4.2 Mirrors

Words to learn

surface   mirror

image   depict

periscope

A smooth, polished **surface**, like that on a **mirror**, is very good at reflecting light.
When you see your face in a mirror, you are seeing light from your face reflecting off the mirror. We call the reflection of your face in the mirror your **image**.

We can show, or **depict**, how light reflects off a mirror in a diagram. We draw straight lines for the beams of light. We show the direction in which the light is travelling with arrows.

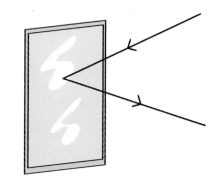

Activity 4.2

Look at your image in one of the mirrors.
Is your image exactly the same as you?
Hold up your left hand. How does this show in the mirror image? Is this what you predicted?
Write a message on a piece of paper. Hold it up to the mirror. How is the mirror image different?
Arrange the two mirrors upright and at right angles to each other. Place your small object where the two mirrors meet.

You will need:
two small mirrors • a small object

Challenge

How many images can you see? Discuss why you think this happens.

Periscopes

A **periscope** is an instrument that uses mirrors.
It allows you to see over the top of something.
This is how a periscope works.

These people are using periscopes to see above the heads of the people in front of them.

Submariners use a periscope to see what is on the surface of the sea. The submarine can remain out of sight below sea level.

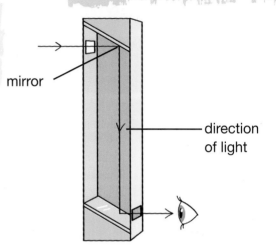

mirror

direction of light

Questions

1 Why does a mirror reflect light well?

2 Draw a diagram to explain how you see your image in a mirror. Depict the light with lines and arrows.

3 Put these statements A, B, C and D, about how a periscope works, in the correct order.

A Light reflects off the bottom mirror into your eye.

B Light travels from a source to the object.

C Light reflects off the object and travels to the top mirror.

D Light reflects off the top mirror and travels down the periscope to the bottom mirror.

Talk about it!

Are all mirror images the same size as the object?

What you have learnt

- Mirrors have a shiny surface which reflects light well.
- A mirror image is back to front.
- A periscope uses mirrors to see things above you.

4.3 Seeing behind you

That's cool! Thanks, Thandi.

Adeline and Thandi are braiding each other's hair. Adeline wants to see what the braids at the back of her head look like. Thandi holds a mirror so that Adeline can see the back of her head.

How can Adeline see the back of her head? The source of light in the room shone on the back of Adeline's head. The light reflected off her head onto the mirror Thandi was holding. The light reflected off Thandi's mirror onto the mirror in front of Adeline. The light reflected off the mirror in front of Adeline into Adeline's eyes.

Activity 4.3

Seeing what is on your back

Draw a picture of something on a sticky note without your partner seeing what you draw. Stick it on your partner's back and ask them what the object in the drawing is. Give your partner two mirrors. They should hold one mirror in front of them and tilt the other mirror in different ways behind them until they can see the picture on their back.

> **You will need:**
> sticky notes • small mirrors

How did the mirrors help your partner to see behind him?

Discuss the way the light travelled.

Look at the pictures. They show different ways that we use mirrors. Discuss how these mirrors help people to see objects that they couldn't see without the mirror.

A security mirror in a shop.

A rear view mirror in a car.

A safety mirror on a bend in the road.

A dentist's mirror.

Questions

1   Imagine you are driving a car. Describe the way the light travels when you see a car behind you in the rear view mirror.

2   Look at the picture of a dentist's mirror. Draw a diagram to depict how the light travels when the dentist uses a mirror to see behind a tooth.

3   How does putting a mirror on a sharp bend help to prevent accidents?

What you have learnt

🌀 Mirrors can help us to see things behind us.

Talk about it!

How could you see what was down the corridor without putting your head out of the door?

Surfaces reflect and absorb light

I can see myself.

I can't see myself at all.

Paulo can see himself in the mirror. The mirror reflects his image back to him. Mateus can't see himself in the wooden chopping board. The wooden surface absorbs light.

All objects reflect light or absorb light. The amount of reflection depends on the surface of the object. A piece of paper, for example, is smooth and flat. However, if you looked at a piece of paper under a microscope, you'd see that it actually contains lots of bumps. Because its surface is not completely smooth, paper absorbs a lot more light than it reflects.

Under a microscope you can see how bumpy the sheet of paper is.

If a surface reflects light very well you will be able to see your reflection in the surface.

Activity 4.4

You will need:
at least six objects

Investigating how well different surfaces reflect light

List the things you are using for your investigation. Some examples are shown on the right.

Predict which surfaces you think will reflect light the best. **Rate** your surfaces beginning with the surface you think will reflect light best. Record your ratings in a list.

Plan and carry out a fair test to see if your prediction was correct. Record your results in a table or a bar chart.

Questions

1 In what ways did you carry out a fair test?
   In what ways was your test unfair?
2 How well did your results support your predictions?
3 What conclusion can you make from your investigation?
   Do you think you need to collect more data to make this conclusion?

What you have learnt

- Flat, shiny surfaces reflect light best.
- Rough surfaces absorb light.

Talk about it!

Before people had mirrors, how do you think they looked at their reflections?

4.5 Light changes direction

How does light travel when it reflects?

The way light reflects off mirrors is very much like the way a ball bounces against a hard surface. If An throws a ball down, it bounces straight back at him. In the second picture, An bounces a ball at an **angle** and it bounces off the floor at the same angle away from him.

An throws the ball straight down.

An throws the ball at an angle.

Light reflects off a mirror in a similar way. In other words, light reflects from a mirror at the same angle as it arrives. The picture shows how light travels when it reflects with lines and arrows. We call a line of light a **ray**.

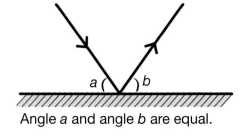

Angle *a* and angle *b* are equal.

Activity 4.5

Demonstrate how light travels when it reflects

Make a small hole with a pin in the middle of the dark paper. Cover the torch glass with the dark paper so that the pin hole is in the middle of the torch glass. Secure the paper with masking tape.

You will need:

a darkened room • a powerful torch a mirror • a sheet of white paper • a piece of dark paper • a pin • some masking tape

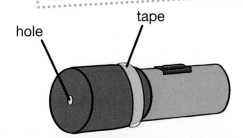

hole

tape

Hold the white paper in front of the mirror about 50 cm away from the mirror.
The mirror must be upright.
Shine your torch at the mirror. You will get a line or ray of light rather than a beam.
Observe the angle at which the ray of light from the torch reaches the mirror.
Observe the point at which the reflected light falls on the paper. Observe the angle that the light reflects off the mirror.
Shine your torch at different angles from the mirror. Observe the rays of light that arrive at the mirror and reflect off the mirror on to the paper.

Questions

1 Draw the path of the beam of light you observed in Activity 4.5. Depict the directions the light rays travelled with lines and arrows.

2 What pattern did you notice about the angle the beam of light arrived at the mirror and the angle it reflected off the mirror? Suggest an explanation for this.

3 Why do you think it was a good idea to repeat the activity several times?

4 The drawing below is incorrect. Redraw it correctly.

What you have learnt

- Light reflects off a mirror at the same angle as it arrives.

Talk about it!

How does the angle of reflection of light affect how you hold a mirror to see behind you?

1 Copy these words. Match up words in column A with their meanings in column B.

Column A	Column B
reflect	a line that light travels in
depict	a place where light comes from
ray	the action of taking something in
light source	show in a certain way
absorb	the action of bouncing off a surface

2 Which surfaces from the list below reflect light and which surfaces absorb light?

> muddy water   mirror   clear water   wood

3 Look at the picture showing Rafaela finding her cat.

a Identify the light source.

b Identify the object.

c Write two sentences to describe how Rafaela sees the cat. Include these words.

> light   torch   travels   eyes   reflects

4 The actress in the picture is getting ready to go on stage. She has three mirrors (1, 2 and 3) tilted at different angles so that she can see behind her. Explain how she can see the back of her head by putting these sentences in the correct order:

1 Light travels to mirror 3.

2 Light reflects off the back of her head to mirror 1.

3 Light reflects off mirror 2.

4 Light reflects off mirror 3 into her eyes.

5 Light from a light source travels to the back of her head.

6 Light travels to mirror 2.

5 Shadows

5.1 Light travels in straight lines

Identify the light sources in these two images.

Light from the Sun travels in straight lines.

Light travels in straight lines from this film projector.

Activity 5.1a

You will need:
a cardboard tube • a torch with cells

Investigating how light travels

Shine your torch down the cardboard tube. Can your partner see the light when they look down the other end of the tube?

Make a bend in the tube. Shine your torch down the tube again. Can your partner see the light when they look down the other end?

Can you explain what you observed?

Questions

1 What **evidence** did you collect about the way light travels?

2 What **conclusion** did you make when you had finished your investigation?

3 Do you think you collected enough evidence to come to this conclusion? Suggest how you could collect more evidence.

Shadows

When light is stopped or **blocked** by some types of solid object, it cannot shine through the object.
A **shadow** forms on the other side of the solid object.

The light from the Sun is blocked by the trees. Shadows are formed.

Activity 5.1b

Observe and make shadows

Go outside and observe the shadows. Make your own shadow.

You will need:
a sunny day

Questions

1 Can you identify the objects blocking the Sun and causing shadows?

2 Draw a picture to show how your own shadow was formed. You need to show the position of the Sun and the position of the shadow.

Talk about it!

If light could travel round corners, would we get shadows?

What you have learnt

🌀 Light travels in straight lines.
🌀 Shadows form when the light is blocked by a solid object.

A shadow forms when light is blocked by an **opaque** object.

When the Sun shines on your back, you see your shadow in front of you. This is because your body does not let any light through it. Materials that do not allow light to pass through are opaque. They form a black shadow.

Some objects are made of materials that allow light to pass through them. Objects that allow all the light to pass through are **transparent**. These do not form any shadow when a light shines on them.

Objects that allow some light to pass through are **translucent**. These form a weak shadow when a light shines on them. The shadow is grey rather than black.

Clear glass is a transparent material. It allows all the light through.

Sunglasses are made of tinted glass. This is a translucent material. It allows some light through, but not all of it.

Shadow shades

| 1 | 2 | 3 | 4 | 5 |

Transparent materials give shade 1 or no shadow. Opaque materials give shade 5 or total shadow. Translucent materials give partial shadows with shades 2, 3 or 4.

Activity 5.2

Investigating which materials let light through

> **You will need:**
> a strong light · a screen · at least six objects made of different materials

Predict the amount of shadow each material will produce when you shine a light. Use the shade key 1–5. Which materials will be opaque? Which will be translucent or transparent? Record your predictions.

Plan and carry out a fair test. Present your results in a bar chart.

Questions

1 Did the results support your predictions? Which materials did not let through the amount of light that you had predicted?
2 How did you make sure that you carried out a fair test?
3 Choose two materials that had shadows of different shades. Explain why the shadows were different shades.

What you have learnt

- Opaque materials do not let light through.
- Translucent materials let some light through.
- Transparent materials let all the light through.

Talk about it!
What things do you use that are made of translucent material?

5.3 Silhouettes and shadow puppets

Words to learn
silhouette   project

What is a silhouette?

An opaque object held between a light source and a screen gives you a shadow on the screen. The shadow of the object is a **silhouette**.

Try making a shadow silhouette of a butterfly with your hands. You will need a light source and a screen.

Join your hands using your thumbs. Your hands are the butterfly's wings.

Try making silhouettes of other things with your hands.

Shadow puppets

A shadow puppet uses a silhouette to represent the puppet.

Long ago, people recorded their history by telling stories. This was before writing was invented. In ancient China and Indonesia, storytellers used shadow puppets to help tell the stories. Each village's storyteller was known as a puppet master. When he put on a show, the whole village would watch. He used his hands and even his feet to make the puppets move. He also added noise effects. To **project** the shadows onto the screen, he hung a bowl of fire above his head.

Sinta Leather Wayang Kulit
Shadow Puppet Indonesia.

Activity 5.3

Make a shadow puppet show

What story are you going to tell? Decide what puppets you need to make. Sketch the shapes. Then trace the shapes on to the cardboard and cut them out with the scissors. Use a hole punch to make eyes and decoration holes.

Fasten sticks to the backs of your puppets with masking tape. Practise acting out the story with your shadow puppets.

Present your shadow puppet show to the class.

Questions

1 Draw a silhouette of a cat.
2 Compare the light source of a traditional Indonesian shadow puppet show with the light source you used for your show.
3 Explain why you could not use clear plastic to make shadow puppets.
4 What properties must a material have to make a good shadow puppet?

Talk about it!
What puppets would you use if you were telling a story about your family?

What you have learnt

- A silhouette is a solid image of a person or a scene, like a shadow. You can make one using black paper.
- Shadow puppets are silhouettes used to make a story on a screen.

5.4 What affects the size of a shadow?

Leila and Alida made a crocodile shadow puppet. If they changed the **position** of their puppet they could make it bigger on the screen. As the crocodile shadow gets bigger it gets scarier!

Activity 5.4

Shadow sizes

Is the size of a shadow affected by changing the position of the object?

You will need:
a light source · a screen · a shadow puppet
a metre rule or a tape measure · some
masking tape · a black pen

Set up the light source and the screen 3 m apart. The distance between light source and the screen is a factor in your investigation. You are not going to change this distance, so we call this the **controlled factor**. The other factor is the distance between the shadow puppet and the light source. You are going to change this.

Stick a piece of masking tape on the floor between the screen and the light source. Mark off the distance every 20 cm from the light source towards the screen for a distance of 2 m. Mark off these distances on the masking tape with a black pen.

Stand at each marked distance. Hold your puppet up so that the light makes a shadow of your puppet on the screen. At each distance, your partner must measure the height of the puppet on the screen and record it.

Repeat all the measurements and record them.

Present your results in a bar line chart.

Questions

1 Identify the factor that you kept the same in your investigation. Identify the factor that you changed.
2 Were your measurements the same the second time? Do you think repeating measurements makes results more reliable?
3 What conclusion have you come to about the size of the shadow and the distance of the object from the light source?

Challenge

Identify **two** other factors in this investigation that you could make the control factor.

What you have learnt

⊚ The size of a shadow is affected by the position of the object.

Talk about it!
What would happen if you changed the position of the screen, but kept the other factors the same?

Words to learn
sundial   noon

What is different about these two shadows?

The shadow of a golf flag at midday.

The shadow of a golf flag late in the afternoon.

Activity 5.5

Investigating the length of a shadow at different times of day

You need:
a sunny day · a stick about 20 cm high
a sheet of white paper · some modelling clay
four stones · a ruler · a marker pen

Choose a place in full sunlight (where there are no shadows nearby) to set up your shadow stick. Push the stick into the ground or stick it upright with modelling clay. Set up your paper and shadow stick like this at 09:00.

(09:00)

You will see that a shadow of the stick falls on the paper. Mark the end of the shadow on the paper with a marker pen and write the time beside the mark. Go outside every hour and mark the end of the shadow and the time. Also observe where the Sun is in the sky each time.

At the end of the afternoon, take the stick down and bring the paper inside. Here is the shadow stick paper used by Aleisha and her friends.

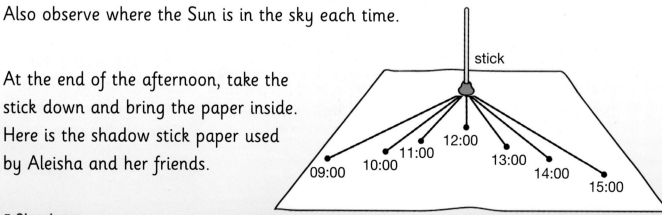

stick

09:00 10:00 11:00 12:00 13:00 14:00 15:00

Join the dots you made for the ends of the shadows to the hole where the stick was. These are your shadow lines. Measure the length of each shadow line with a ruler. Record the lengths of the shadows in a table alongside the times. Repeat this experiment over several days, using a different sheet of paper each day.

Questions

1 Draw a picture of the shadows you recorded. Show the way the length and direction of the shadows changed. Label the times.

2 What did you notice about the position of the Sun at different times of day? Was it low in the sky or high in the sky? How did this affect the position of the shadow at different times of day?

3 What pattern did you notice about the length of the shadow and the time of day?

Challenge

Compare the measurements for the same times of the day on different days. Explain any differences.

People told the time by **sundials** before they had clocks. When the Sun was directly overhead and the shadow was shortest, it was **noon**.

A sundial. The position of the shadow tells the time.

Talk about it!

Would you get the same measurements if you did the shadow stick experiment in three months' time?

What you have learnt

🌀 Shadows change in length and position throughout the day.

🌀 We can tell the time using a sundial or a shadow stick.

5.6 Measuring light intensity

Light intensity is a measure of the amount of light in an area. In the past, people measured light intensity in 'candlepower'. This was the amount of light given out by a candle. Today people measure light intensity with light meters.

A digital light meter measures light intensity.

Activity 5.6

Measure light intensity

You will need:
a light meter • a candle • a light bulb and an LED bulb • a book • measuring tape

If you have a digital light meter, measure the light intensity. You will need to measure outside in the sun, outside in the shade, inside the classroom and in a dark cupboard. Record the measurements.

Design your own way of comparing the light intensity given out by a candle, a light bulb and an LED. Predict which light sources will give the best light intensity.

To test your prediction, measure how far away from each light source you can see well enough to read. Record your results. Compare the light intensity from these three light sources.

Questions

1 Think about your comparison of light intensity. How well did your results support your predictions?

2 How did you make your test fair?

People who need to measure light intensity

The pictures show people who need to measure light intensity.

Many flowers and vegetables grown are grown in commercial greenhouses. Inside a greenhouse the temperature, amount of moisture and the light intensity are controlled.

Film makers must make sure the light intensity is exactly right for filming.

Test match cricket has to be played in daylight. When the light intensity falls to a certain level the day's play comes to an end.

Question

1   Explain why people need to control light intensity in a commercial greenhouse.

What you have learnt

- Light intensity can be measured using a light meter.

Talk about it!
How does light intensity affect how you take photographs?

For hundreds of years, scientists have tried to explain and understand the things that they observed about light. One scientist would have an idea about light, and then another scientist would collect new evidence and change the idea.

Words to learn
prism   refraction

Rainbows

You can see a rainbow when drops of water in the air are hit by sunlight at a certain angle.

You see a rainbow when the Sun is shining and it is raining.

Activity 5.7

Making a rainbow using sunlight

Put a sprinkler on a garden hose.
Go outside on a sunny day. Turn on the water and observe the rainbows.

You will need:
a garden hose with a sprinkler attached
glasses of water

Line up glasses of water on a table, near a window facing the sun. The sunlight passes through the water to make rainbows on the other side of the glasses. Rainbows will appear either on the wall or floors, depending on the position and the direction of the sun.

How did scientists explain rainbows?

Aristotle was a Greek scientist who lived in the fourth century BCE. He thought rainbows were caused by clouds reflecting sunlight at certain angles.

500 years later, the Islamic scientist, Ibn al-Haytham, thought the rainbow was like a reflection in a mirror. The cloud was like the mirror, with the sunlight reflecting off the cloud.

About 950 years ago, Shen Kuo, from China, suggested that the sunlight hit the rain to make rainbows.

The English scientist, Isaac Newton, was the first to explain the rainbow accurately, about 300 years ago. He showed that sunlight (also called white light) is made up of different colours. Our eyes don't see these colours separately.

Newton used a **prism** to demonstrate that white light is a mix of colours. When sunlight passes through a prism, it bends. This is called **refraction**. The angle of bending is different for the various colours of light: red, orange, yellow, green, blue, indigo and violet.

In a rainbow, every raindrop acts as a tiny prism. The Sun shines through the raindrops and light is refracted, giving a rainbow.

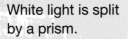
White light is split by a prism.

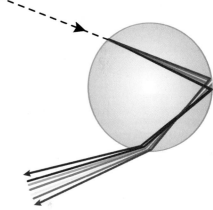
Red light is refracted at a bigger angle than violet light.

Questions

1 Name **two** scientists who thought that rainbows were caused by reflection.
2 What did Newton use to obtain new evidence about how rainbows form?
3 What evidence did Newton collect that changed ideas about how rainbows form?

Talk about it!
What shape do rainbows make in the sky?

What you have learnt

- Scientists have ideas to explain things. Scientists base their ideas on observations and evidence from experiments they do.
- Ideas have changed about light over hundreds of years.

5 Check your progress

1 Use the following words in a sentence to describe how a shadow forms.

> shadow   light   light source   object   blocked   opaque

2 Here is a list of materials.

> clear plastic wrap   tin foil   clear glass   wooden block   tinted glass

a Choose **two** of the materials that are opaque.

b Choose **two** of the materials that are translucent.

c Choose **one** of the materials that is transparent.

3 Chad is making a shadow puppet show. He cut out his puppet from cardboard and stuck it on a stick. But the shadow was too big for his screen.

a What is Chad using for a light source?

b What is Chad using for a screen?

c Describe **two** ways in which Chad could make the shadow smaller.

4 Some children did a shadow stick experiment. Copy and complete these sentences about shadow length at different times of the day. Choose the correct alternatives.

a Between 08:00 and midday the shadow becomes shorter/longer.

b Between midday and 16:00 the shadow becomes shorter/longer.

c The shadow is longest/shortest at sunrise and sunset.

d The shadow is longest/shortest in the middle of the day.

5 Emilio and Julio are travelling by car through a tunnel. The tunnel is 10 km long. At first it is completely dark in the tunnel. Then, after 5 minutes Julio says, 'look, I can see the light at the end of the tunnel!'.

Explain why the boys could not see the light at the end of the tunnel to begin with.

6 Earth's movements

6.1 The Sun, the Earth and the Moon

What are the Sun, the Earth and the Moon?

A camera on the **spacecraft** Galileo took this image of the Earth and the Moon on its way to explore the **planet** Jupiter. The image shows us that the Moon is much smaller than the Earth and that they are surrounded by black, empty space. The Sun lights up part of the Earth and the Moon. The Sun is shining because it is a **star**. All stars give out light. Earth is a planet. Planets reflect the light of the Sun. The Moon also reflects the light of the Sun.

The Earth and the Moon are constantly moving in space. But they make the same movements all the time. The Moon moves around the Earth and the Earth moves around the Sun.

The Earth and the Moon.

Activity 6.1

Model the movements of the Earth and the Moon

In the model, the football represents the Sun, the tennis ball represents the Earth and the marble represents the Moon.

Place the 'Sun' in the centre of a large table or open space. Do not move the 'Sun'.

One person moves the 'Earth' slowly in an oval path around the 'Sun'. This represents Earth's **orbit** around the Sun. Another person should move the 'Moon' quickly in an oval path around the 'Earth'. This represents the Moon's orbit around the Earth.

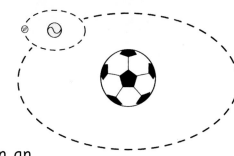

Questions

1 What is an orbit and what shape is it?
2 How does the Earth move in relation to the Sun?
3 Explain the difference between a star and a planet.
4 Copy the diagram and add these labels:
   Sun
   Earth
   Moon
   Earth's orbit around the Sun
   Moon's orbit around the Earth

Challenge

Find out about the spacecraft Galileo using the internet.

Make a poster to show what you find out.

What you have learnt

- The Earth moves around the Sun in an orbit.
- The Moon moves around the Earth in an orbit.

Talk about it!
Would we be able to live on Earth if the Sun wasn't there?

6.2 Does the Sun move?

Words to learn

appears to

Serena wakes up early because the Sun shines through her window. In the afternoon, no Sun shines through Serena's window. Has the Sun moved?

Activity 6.2a

Tracking the Sun on the window

Observe where the Sun shines through your classroom window in the early morning.
Put up a sticker on the window every hour to mark the spot where the Sun shines through.
Record the date and time on each sticker.
Repeat this activity every day for two weeks if the day is sunny.

You will need:
some stickers • a sunny day

Safety Never look directly at the Sun.
You will damage your eyes.

Questions

1 Draw the pattern you observed when you tracked the Sun on the window.
2 Based on the observations and measurements you made over two weeks, predict how this pattern might continue in the weeks ahead.

Although the Sun **appears to** move across the window it doesn't really move. In fact it is the Earth that moves. Let's test this idea.

Activity 6.2b

You will need:
a strong lamp

A model to show that the Sun does not move

Place the lamp on a table and turn it on. This represents the Sun shining.

Stand in a circle with everyone facing outwards. The circle represents the Earth. Move round slowly so that each person faces the Sun in turn.

Keep moving until you reach the spot where you started.

Collect evidence to support the idea that the Earth moves throughout the day and not the Sun.

Observe when you are facing the Sun, when the Sun is on your left side, when the Sun is on your right side and when you can't see the Sun at all.

In the next topic, we will look more closely at how the Earth moves.

Questions

1   In this activity, was the 'Earth' or the 'Sun' moving?
2   What time of day was it when you:
    a faced the 'Sun'   b had your back to the 'Sun'
    c could see the 'Sun' on your left side.
3   Do you think you collected enough evidence to test the idea that the Earth moves throughout the day and not the Sun?

What you have learnt

- The Sun appears to move across the sky during the day.
- The Sun does not really move but the Earth moves.

Talk about it!
Does the Moon move across the sky?

6.3 The Earth rotates on its axis

The **globe** is a model of the Earth. It is shaped like a ball and it has a stick passing through it from the North Pole to the South Pole. This stick represents the Earth's **axis**. In space, the Earth is not upright. It is **tilted** on its axis like the globe.

The Earth **spins** all the time on its axis, from west to east. We call this movement **rotation**. The Earth completes one rotation on its axis every 24 hours.

Find your country on the globe. Put a piece of tape on your country. Now spin the globe on its axis and watch your country go round and round. This movement happens all the time, but we do not notice it.

Imagine that you are in a vehicle that is moving very fast. You might be travelling at 120 km/h, which seems fast, but the Earth is rotating on its axis at least ten times faster than this!

Activity 6.3

Use a model to show day and night

You will need:
a globe · a sticker · a torch

The torch represents the Sun and the globe represents the Earth. Shine the torch on the globe. This represents the Sun shining on the Earth. Now spin the globe from west to east in an anticlockwise direction.

Observe which part of the 'Earth' is lit up. Can the whole 'Earth' be lit up at one time?

Now place a sticker on the 'Earth'. Continue to shine the torch on the 'Earth'. Spin the 'Earth' and watch the sticker.

Is the sticker lit up by the torch all the time? As the 'Earth' spins, say 'day' when the light shines on the sticker and 'night' when no light shines on the sticker.

Questions

1   Copy and complete this sentence.
    The Earth's _____ on its axis causes everywhere on the Earth's surface to experience _____ and _____ over a period of 24 hours.

2   Copy the diagram and shade the half of the Earth having night black and the half having day yellow.

Sun's

rays

3   You are going to explain the idea of night and day to a younger learner. Plan how you could explain this using things that you could find at home.

Challenge

Uwe lives in Germany. Brad lives in Canada. If Uwe wants to contact Brad he should phone when it is evening in Germany. Why shouldn't he phone Brad when it is morning in Germany?

Talk about it!
What would it be like if the Earth completed one rotation every 10 hours?

What you have learnt

🌀 Earth rotates on its axis from west to east.

🌀 Earth completes one rotation every 24 hours.

6.4 Sunrise and sunset

The **horizon** is the line between the Earth and the sky. Look at the horizon in the east, where the Sun rises, in the early morning. The Sun appears to rise above the horizon. We call this **sunrise**.

During the day, the Sun appears to move higher and higher in the sky. In the afternoon, the Sun appears to get lower in the sky. In the evening, the Sun appears to sink below the horizon in the west. We call this **sunset**.

A sunrise.

The Sun is not really moving across the sky as it appears to do. It is the Earth's rotation that causes sunrise and sunset. Remember that the Earth rotates once every 24 hours. Does the Sun rise and set at the same time every day?

Activity 6.4

Investigating the times of sunrise and sunset in Cape Town, South Africa

Date	Sunrise	Sunset	Length of day	Difference
1 Feb 2013	06:08	19:51	13h 43m	
2 Feb 2013	06:09	19:51	13h 42m	–1 m
3 Feb 2013	06:10	19:50	13h 40m	
4 Feb 2013	06:11	19:49	13h 39m	
5 Feb 2013	06:12	19:48	13h 37m	
6 Feb 2013	06:13	19:47	13h 35m	
7 Feb 2013	06:14	19:46	13h 33m	
Date	**Sunrise**	**Sunset**	**Length of day**	**Difference**
14 Mar 2013	06:45	19:06	12h 21m	
15 Mar 2013	06:46	19:04	12h 18m	–3 m
16 Mar 2013	06:46	19:03	12h 17m	
17 Mar 2013	06:47	19:01	12h 14m	
18 Mar 2013	06:48	19:00	12h 12m	
19 Mar 2013	06:49	18:59	12h 10m	
20 Mar 2013	06:50	18:57	12h 08m	

Look at the times of sunrise and sunset. You find the length of day by subtracting the sunrise time from the sunset time.

Is there is a difference in the length of day from one day to the next?

Work out the difference in the lengths of day between 3 February 2013 and 7 February 2013. Repeat these calculations for the period between 16 March 2013 and 20 March 2013.

Collect data for sunrise and sunset times for a week where you live. Present the data in a table. Draw bar line charts to show your data.

Questions

1 Between 3 February and 20 March are the days in Cape Town getting longer or shorter?

2 a Predict how the length of day will change during the month of April.
  b How could you test your prediction?

3 Compare the pattern of changing length of day in Cape Town with the pattern of changing length of day where you live.

Challenge

Predict how you think the length of day will change in Cape Town from May until the end of the year.

How could you collect sufficient evidence to test this idea?

Talk about it!

Why do you think the length of day changes?

What you have learnt

- The Sun appears to rise in the east and set in the west.
- Sunrise and sunset times and the length of day change every day throughout the year.

6.5 The Earth revolves around the Sun

What happens in a **year** in your family?
What does our planet do in one year?

The Earth travels around or revolves around the Sun. The Earth takes $365\frac{1}{4}$ days, or one year, to complete one **revolution**. It travels in an oval-shaped orbit. As it travels around the Sun, it also spins on its axis.

Activity 6.5

Model the Earth's revolution

Work in a group. Stand in a large oval shape.
This represents the orbit of the Earth around
the Sun. Each of you represents Earth at a different
position in the orbit. One person stands in the centre
of the oval and represents the Sun.
Each person in the 'orbit' should walk around
the 'Sun'. As you walk around the 'Sun', you should
also turn on the spot.

Question

1 Which movements of the Earth were you showing when you:
   a turned on the spot
   b walked around the 'Sun'?

Length of day and changing seasons

In Topic 6.4, you saw that the length of day changed from one day to the next. The length of day either gets longer or shorter. This change in the length of day is a sign that the season was changing. The seasons are caused by the Earth revolving around the Sun once a year and the tilting of the Earth's axis.

The diagram shows the position of the Earth in its orbit around the Sun at different months of the year.

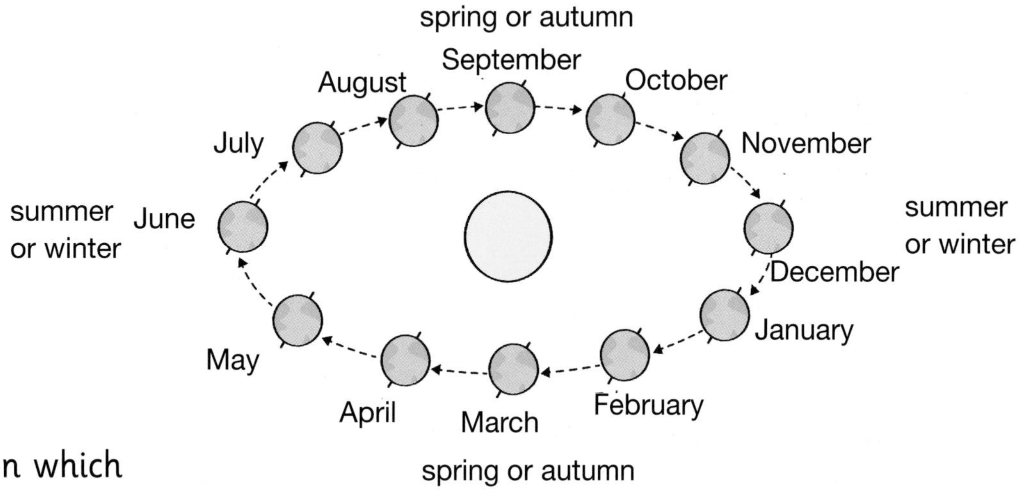

spring or autumn
September
August   October
July   November
summer or winter   June   summer or winter
May   December
                    January
April   March   February
spring or autumn

The seasons depend on which **hemisphere** you live in. Countries between the equator and the North Pole are in the northern hemisphere. Countries between the equator and the South Pole are in the southern hemisphere. When the northern hemisphere has summer the southern hemisphere has winter.

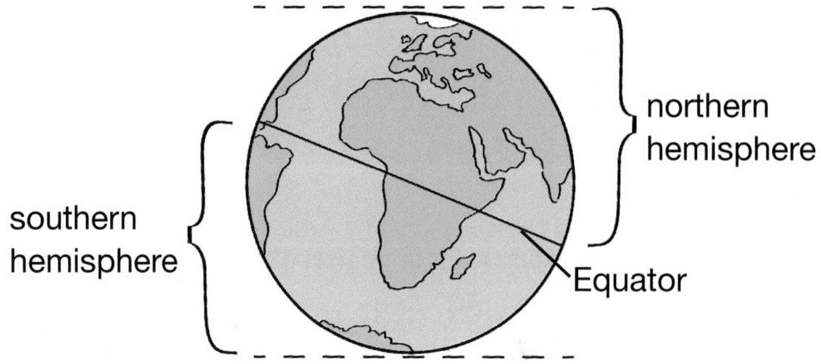

northern hemisphere

southern hemisphere

Equator

This is because the northern hemisphere is tilted towards the Sun. In summer, the days are long and the nights are short. At the equator, there are no distinct seasons – there is equal day and night on every day of the year.

Questions

1 a Explain why this image is showing summer in the southern hemisphere and not the northern hemisphere.

   b Suggest the length of day experienced at A, B and C.

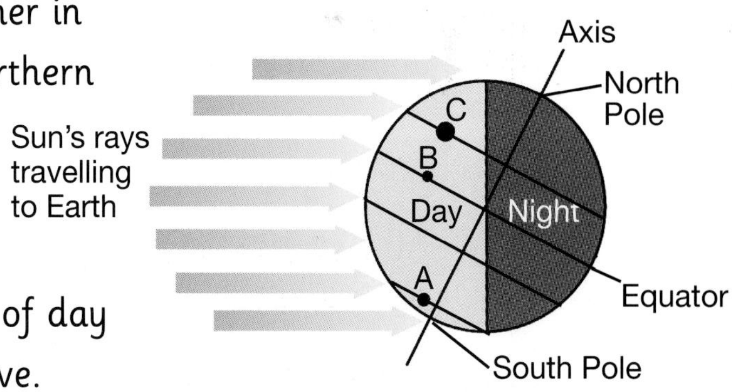

2 a Describe the changing pattern of length of day between January and June where you live.

   b Suggest an explanation for this pattern based on your scientific knowledge.

Axis
North Pole
C
B
Sun's rays travelling to Earth
Day   Night
A
Equator
South Pole

What you have learnt

☼ The Earth revolves around the Sun in an orbit once every $365\frac{1}{4}$ days. As it revolves, it spins on its axis.

Talk about it!
If the Earth was not tilted on its axis, would we have seasons?

6.6 Exploring the solar system

Words to learn

solar system   comet

asteroid   meteor

astronomer   astronaut

The **solar system** consists of the Sun, which is a star, and eight planets. The diagram shows the solar system.

Earth is one of the planets. All the planets revolve around the Sun. There are also many moons. Our Moon is one of these.

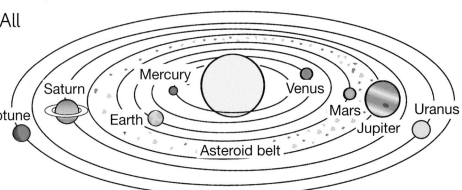

A **comet** is a lump of ice and dirt that moves in a large orbit around the Sun. Between Mars and Jupiter are rocky objects called **asteroids** that orbit the Sun. When rocks and particles from space enter Earth's atmosphere, we call them **meteors** or shooting stars.

How scientists discovered the solar system

An Egyptian **astronomer**, called Ptolemy, described how the Moon, Sun, planets and stars revolved around Earth. The Indian astronomers, Varahamihira and Bramagupta supported the concept of a spherical Earth and planets. The astronomer Aryabhata (476–550 CE) agreed that the Earth was spherical, and stated that the apparent rotation of the planets was a result of the actual rotation of the Earth.

500 years ago, a Polish astronomer, called Copernicus, observed the movements of the planets and decided that Ptolemy was wrong. He wrote a book saying that the Earth and all other planets moved around the Sun. For a long time nobody believed him!

400 years ago, the Italian astronomer, Galileo, used the newly invented telescope to study the sky. He noticed that Venus had different sides lit up by the Sun at different times. This means that Venus must move around the Sun. Galileo agreed with Copernicus.

Activity 6.6

Research the life and discoveries of an astronomer

Choose an astronomer. Use the internet or library books to find out more about their life and discoveries.

Share your findings with the class.

Discovering more about the solar system

In the 1960s, there was the 'Space Race' between the USA and Russia to send an **astronaut** to land on the Moon. Amazing new equipment has increased our recent knowledge.

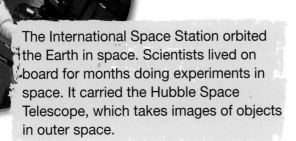

The International Space Station orbited the Earth in space. Scientists lived on board for months doing experiments in space. It carried the Hubble Space Telescope, which takes images of objects in outer space.

Probes are unmanned spacecraft that travel to different planets and moons. They are controlled from a control centre on Earth. Space probes take images and gather information.

Questions

1. Draw a diagram of the solar system that Ptolemy described.
2. Describe the evidence that Copernicus and Galileo collected to prove that the Sun was at the centre of the solar system.
3. Imagine a new project to discover more about Saturn. What equipment will help scientists find out more?

What you have learnt

🌀 Over the last 2000 years, ideas about the solar system have changed as new evidence is gathered.

Talk about it!
Why do you think astronauts have never visited Saturn or Jupiter?

6.7 Exploring the stars

What is the universe?

The **universe** is the whole of space. It contains billions of stars in huge groups. Each group is called a **galaxy**. Our solar system is a tiny part of one of these galaxies called the Milky Way.

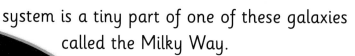

A star cluster in the Milky Way galaxy. This cluster contains hundreds of thousands of stars, each one as big as or bigger than our Sun.

Until 100 years ago, astronomers thought that the universe was not much bigger than the Milky Way galaxy. Then an American astronomer, Edwin Hubble, began to study a distant cloud of gas with a powerful telescope. He discovered that the cloud was a mass of stars. This meant it was another galaxy. Soon many more galaxies were discovered and it became clear that the universe is gigantic.

Hubble wanted to find out whether the universe was getting bigger or not. By observation through telescopes over many years, he realised that the universe was **expanding**.

Activity 6.7

Making a model of the expanding universe

You will need:
a balloon • a rubber band • stickers

Partly blow up the balloon and tie the end with a rubber band so that no air escapes. Place a few stickers over the balloon. Take off the rubber band and blow the balloon up more. Tie the end of the balloon with the rubber band. Observe what has happened to the stickers.

Telescopes

The most important instrument for looking at the stars is the **optical telescope**. This makes distant objects like stars look bigger and brighter. Mirrors inside the telescopes collect and **focus** the light to make images.

The mirrors on The Hobby-Eberly Telescope at the McDonald Observatory, Texas, America.

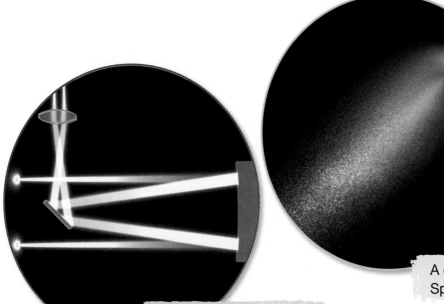

Light inside a telescope.

A comet observed by the Hubble Space Telescope (HST).

Questions

1   **a** In the model from Activity 6.7, what does the balloon represent and what do the stickers represent?

   b How does the model show that the universe is expanding?

2   How did Edwin Hubble collect evidence that the universe was expanding?

3   Use library books and the internet to find out about the Hubble Space Telescope.

Talk about it!

What problems would you have to solve on a trip into space?

What you have learnt

🌀 Astronomers research the universe and collect evidence using powerful telescopes.

1

a   Copy the diagram below. Write the following labels on the diagram.

| Sun   Earth   Moon   orbit   axis   rotation   revolution |

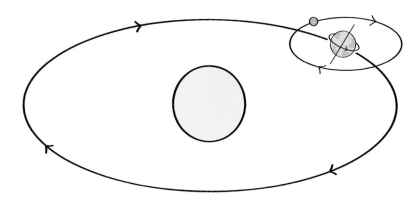

b   Which Earth movement causes day and night?

c   Which two factors cause the seasons?

2   Here are some data for sunrise and sunset times for Kingston, Jamaica in January 2012.

Date	Sunrise	Sunset	Length of day
1 January	06:38	17:43	
4 January	06:39	17:45	
8 January	06:40	17:47	
12 January	06:41	17:50	
16 January	06:42	17:52	
20 January	06:42	17:55	

a   Copy and complete the table by filling in the length of day.
b   Describe the pattern of change in the length of day.
c   Which season do you think Kingston is having in January?
d   Which season will Kingston experience in six months' time? Explain why.

3   a   List **three** pieces of equipment that have helped astronomers to discover more about the solar system and the stars.
b   Write a sentence about each piece of equipment to describe what it does.

4   This is an image of a rover on the surface of Mars. A rover is a small vehicle worked by robots. They have been used on the Moon and Mars to collect samples of rock, take photographs and conduct experiments.

a   How does the rover get to Mars?
b   What or who operates the rover?
c   What kind of information does it collect?

Reference

This section of the Learner's Book covers some of the new scientific enquiry skills for this stage. They build on the skills already gained from previous stages. You should refer to these skills whenever you need them.

Measuring the volume of a liquid

Measuring cylinders come in different sizes. Choose one that is the right size for the volume of liquid you want to measure.

Put the measuring cylinder on a table.

Count the lines between two numbers. On some measuring cylinders each line is 1 ml. On others it can be 2 ml or even 5 ml.

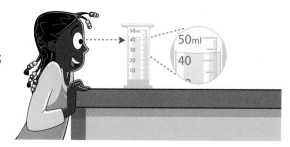

Put your eye level with the top of the liquid to read the scale.

Shona measures 43 ml of water

The top of the liquid may curve. Measure to the bottom of the curve. This measuring cylinder contains 43 ml of liquid.

Choosing a bar chart or a line graph

Use a bar chart when your results are different objects or different groups with a number for each one. The bars are separate because each bar shows a different object or group, for example, type of fruit.

Fruit	Seeds
Apple	5
Orange	10
Kiwi	30

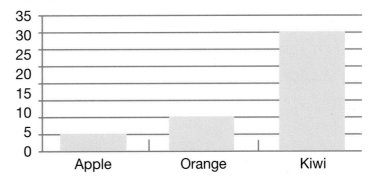

Light source	Brightness at 10 cm
Torch	80 lux
Lamp	300 lux
Candle	20 lux

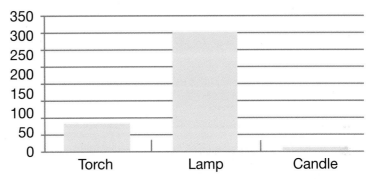

Use line graphs when your results are pairs of numbers.

Line graphs can be used to show how something changes with time such as an increase in temperature or plant height.

Here hot water is cooling.

Time in minutes	0	2	4	6
Temperature of water in °C	60	35	25	20

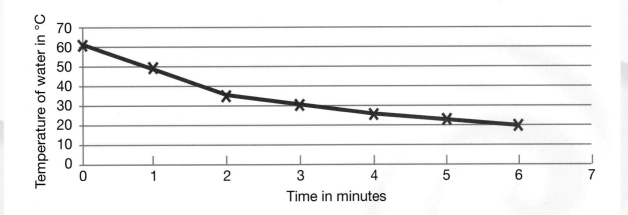

How to draw a line graph

Eva is measuring the length of a shadow at different times.

These are her results.

Time in hours	10.00	11.00	12.00	13.00	14.00
Length of shadow in cm	90	45	25	50	85

Eva wants to draw a line graph.

First she has to draw the axes.

She looks at the longest shadow length (90 cm). She draws the y axis up to 100 cm.

There are 5 different times to go on the x axis. The times are all 1 hour apart. She draws a line for the x axis.

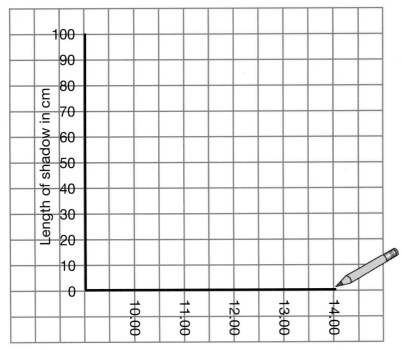

Time in hours

Eva uses a ruler to draw straight lines.

She writes the numbers so that the lines on the graph paper go through the middle of the numbers.

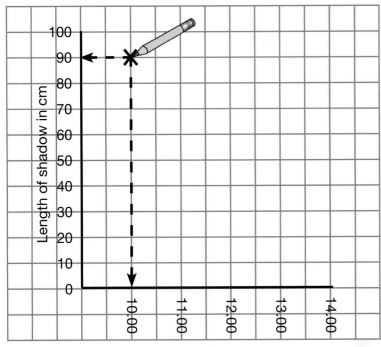

Time in hours

Now Eva needs to plot the results on the graph.

The first result is 90 cm at 10.00.
She finds the line on the graph for 10.00.
She finds the line on the graph for 90 cm.
She makes a cross where the two lines meet.

Next Eva finds the line on the graph for 11.00 and the line for 45 cm. She draws a cross where the two lines meet.

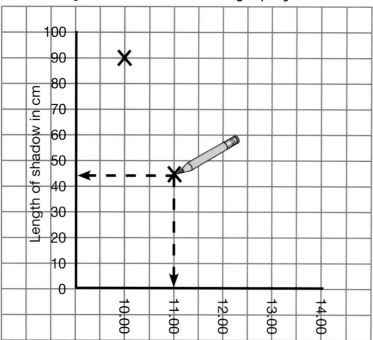

She plots all the results the same way.

Then she draws a line that goes through the crosses on the graph.

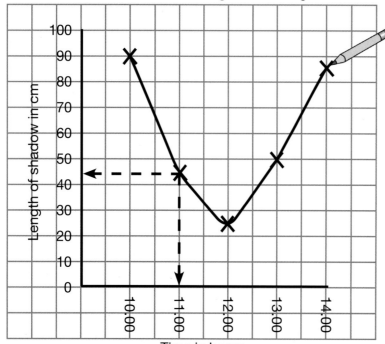

The graph shows that the shadow gets shorter until 12.00.

After that it gets longer.

Repeating measurements to make results more reliable

Song and Mansi have a question: 'Will a paper towel that is twice as wet take twice as long to dry?'

Mansi puts five drops of water onto one paper towel. Song puts ten drops on another.

They put both the paper towels on a radiator. They use a stopwatch to time how long they take to dry.

But it's hard to tell exactly when it's dry! We can repeat our measurements.

Yes, that would make our results more reliable.

A reliable result is a result that is close to the true answer.

They decide to repeat their measurements.

Number of drops	5	10
1 Time to dry in minutes	13	15
2 Time to dry in minutes	12	20

Mansi's two measurements are similar. Song's are not. To find out which of his results is the most reliable he can repeat the measurement again.

Akiko and Sasha are investigating the question: 'Does the shape of a container affect how fast water evaporates?'

They have 500 ml of water in each container. They measure how much water is left in each container every day.

Here are their results.

Day	1	2	3	4	5
Water left in measuring cylinder in ml	498	496	495	493	490
Water left in measuring jug in ml	452	408	445	311	250

Look carefully at the results.
The water is evaporating so the numbers should be getting smaller.

445 ml on day three is wrong. It has gone up from 408 ml on day two!

But 408 ml on day two could be wrong.

They decide to repeat the measurements to check.

Day	1	2	3	4	5
Water left in measuring jug in ml	454	410	345	310	253

The new results look correct.
The measurement of 445 ml on day 3 was wrong.

Glossary and index

		Page
absorb	to take in a substance	8
angle	the number of degrees between a horizontal and a line	62
anther	tip of the stamen	24
appears to	when it looks as though something has caused an action but in fact it was caused by something else	84
asteroid	body smaller than a moon that orbits the Sun	92
astronaut	a person who travels in space	93
astronomer	a scientist who studies the universe	92
axis	an imaginary line passing through Earth from the North Pole to the South Pole; Earth rotates around this axis	86
beam	a band that light travels in	54
blocked	stopped continuing on its way	67
boil	when water changes from a liquid to a gas at a high temperature	46
boiling point	the temperature at which a liquid boils	46
carpel	female part of a flower	24
comet	lump of ice and dirt that moves in a large orbit around the Sun	92
conclusion	the decision you come to when you have all the evidence	66
condensation	when a gas changes to a liquid	42
controlled factor	the factor that does not change in an experiment or investigation	72
crystal	a small piece of solid substance with a regular shape, such as sugar and salt; some crystals can dissolve in water	40

depict	show in a certain way	56
dissolve	when a substance mixes with another substance and becomes part of it	40
embryo	the tiny plant inside a seed that can grow into new plant	6
energy	quantity needed to make things happen	34
evaporation	when a liquid turns into a gas	34
evidence	information gained from an experiment or investigation	66
expand	get larger	94
explode	to burst open with a lot of force	23
factor	a variable in an investigation or experiment	12
fertilisation	the process that joins the pollen and eggs to make seeds	27
focus	concentrate on	95
galaxy	a huge mass of stars	94
germination	when a seed starts to grow	8
globe	a model of Earth	86
hemisphere	half the Earth, for example, the northern hemisphere is between the equator and the North Pole	91
horizon	the line where the sky meets the Earth	88
image	the picture of the object that you see on a screen or in a mirror	56
life cycle	the different stages in a plant's life from when it grows from a seed until it makes its own seeds	30
light intensity	the amount of light in an area	76
light source	a place where light comes from, for example, the Sun or a torch	54

melts	when a solid changes to a liquid	48
melting point	the temperature at which a solid melts	48
meteor	bits of rock and sand that enter Earth's atmosphere from space	92
mirror	a very smooth, shiny surface that reflects light well	56
nectar	a sweet liquid that flowers make	26
noon	12:00, midday	75
object	the thing that is reflected	55
opaque	does not allow light to pass through	68
optical telescope	an instrument containing mirrors and lenses that make distant objects like stars look bigger and brighter	95
orbit	the path taken when a body moves around a larger body in space	83
ovary	part of a plant that contains eggs	24
periscope	an instrument with tilted mirrors that allows you to see over the top of something	57
planet	a body in space that revolves around a star	82
pollen	yellow or brown powder made in the stamen	24
pollination	the process that brings pollen from the stamen to the stigma of a flower	26
position	the placing of something in relation to things around it	72
prism	a three-dimensional object made of transparent material	79
project	to send out	70
rate	put in order (for example, from best to worst)	61
ray	a line that light travels in	62
reflect	the action of bouncing off a surface	55

refraction	the bending of light when it passes from one material to another	79
reproduce	to form young	19
reverse	when something happens in the opposite order or direction	42
revolution	the movement of a planet around the Sun in an orbit or any other body in the universe moving around a bigger body	90
rotation	the movement of a body on its axis	86
scent	the smell that flower petals give out	18
seed	part of a plant that can grow into a new plant	6
seed coat	the outer cover that protects the seed	7
seed dispersal	when seeds are spread or scattered away from the plant where they formed	20
seedlings	the new plant that grows from a germinated seed	20
sepals	outer ring of small green leaves on the base of a flower	24
shadow	forms when light is blocked by some types of solid object	67
shrivel	to become small and very dry	8
silhouette	the shadow that forms when you hold an opaque object between a light source and a screen	70
solar system	the Sun with eight planets and other bodies such as dwarf planets, moons, and asteroids revolving round it	92
solute	the material that is dissolved	40
solution	a mixture usually made of a solid dissolved in a liquid	40
solvent	the liquid in which the solute dissolves	40
spacecraft	a machine launched into space by a rocket	82

spin	a fast rotation movement	86
spongy	like a sponge with lots of holes in it that can be filled with air or water	22
stamen	male part of a flower	24
star	a body in space that gives off light and heat	82
steam	the hot mist produced when water boils; it is made of hot condensing water vapour	46
stigma	tip of the carpel	24
sundial	a shadow stick used to tell the time before there were clocks	75
sunrise	the time when the Sun appears to rise over the horizon	88
sunset	the time when the Sun appears to sink below the horizon	88
surface	the top layer that is next to the air	56
tilted	at an angle, not vertical	86
transluscent	allows some light to pass through	68
transparent	allows all the light to pass through	68
universe	the whole of space	94
volume	the amount of space a substance takes up in a container	38
water cycle	when water evaporates from seas, rivers and lakes, condenses to form clouds, and falls back to Earth as rain	44
water vapour	the gas formed when liquid water changes into a gas	34
wither	to dry out and start to die	19
year	the length of time it takes Earth to complete one revolution around the Sun	90

Acknowledgements

The authors and publisher are grateful for the permissions granted to reproduce copyright materials. While every effort has been made, it has not always been possible to identify the sources of all the materials used, or to trace all the copyright holders.

If any omissions are brought to our notice, we will be happy to include the appropriate acknowledgements on reprinting.

The publisher is grateful to the experienced teachers Mansoora Shoaib Shah, Lahore Grammar School, 55 Main, Gulberg, Lahore and Lynne Ransford for their careful reviewing of the content.

p. 6*tl* Matt1234/ iStockphoto; p. 6*bl* Pablo Caridad/Hemera/ Thinkstock; p. 6*tr* ashleigh kirkham/iStock/ Thinkstock; p. 6*br* joannawnuk/ Shutterstock; p. 8 YuryZap/ Shutterstock; p. 12 Olga Lipatova/ Shutterstock; p. 17*l* Nigel Cattlin/ Alamy; p. 17*r* Nigel Cattlin/ Alamy; p. 18*tl* SH-Vector/ Shutterstock; p. 18*tc* sakhorn/ Shutterstock; p. 18*tr* Claudia Carlsen/ Shutterstock; p. 18*bl* Irina Borsuchenko/ Shutterstock; p. 18*br* enna van duinen/iStock/ Thinkstock; p. 21*l* MVPhoto/ Shutterstock; p. 21*r* Joe Blossom/ Alamy; p. 21*c* Alon Meir/ Alamy; p. 22*tl* Borges Samuel/ Alamy; p. 22*tcr* joannawnuk/ Shutterstock; p. 22*tr* William Radcliffe/RGB Ventures LLC dba SuperStock/ Alamy; p. 22*tcl* Neil Lucas/ Nature Picture Library; p. 22*br* Martin Shields/ Alamy; p. 23*t* Kathy Coatney/AgStock Images, Inc./ Alamy; p. 23*b* AfriPics.com/ Alamy; p. 25 Vladimir Wrangel/ Shutterstock; p. 26*t* Elliotte Rusty Harold/ Shutterstock; p. 26*b* Tim Gainey/ Alamy; p. 28*l* merrilyanne/iStock/ Thinkstock; p. 28*c* Christian Musat/iStock/ Thinkstock; p. 28*r* Itsik Marom/ Alamy; p. 29 Phent/ Shutterstock; p. 33*l* Custom Life Science Images/ Alamy; p. 33*r* Africa Studio/ Shutterstock; p. 36*tr* Edwin Jimenez/Image Source/ Alamy; p. 36*bl* Margoe Edwards/ Shutterstock; p. 37*tl* GoodMood Photo/ Shutterstock; p. 37*tr* TMI/ Alamy; p. 37*br* Svetlana Lukienko/ Shutterstock; p. 40 Matin Siepmann/imagebroker / Shutterstock; p. 41 Gyro Photography/a. collection/amana images inc./ Alamy; p. 42 gresei/ Shutterstock; p. 48*tr* Jochen Tack/ Alamy; p. 48*bl* silver-john/ Shutterstock; p. 48*bc* Palle Christensen/ Shutterstock; p. 48*br* Artem Merzlenko/ Alamy; p. 51 You Touch Pix of EuToch/ Shutterstock; p. 54 AlinaMD/ iStock/ Thinkstock; p. 57*r* Danny Bird/ Alamy; p. 57*l* Al Messerschmidt/Getty Images Sport/ Getty Images; p. 59*tr* motion picture library/ paul ridsdale/ Alamy; p. 59*br* MedicImage/ Alamy; p. 59*bl* Stan Kujawa/ Alamy; p. 59*tl* AFP/ Getty Images; p. 60 Custom Life Science Images/ Alamy; p. 66*l* Markus Gann/ Shutterstock; p. 66*r* Pixel 4 Images/ Shutterstock; p. 67 Leonid Ikan/ Shutterstock; p. 68*l* Andrey tiyk/ Shutterstock; p. 68*r* Purestock/ Thinkstock; p. 70 Doug Steley A / Alamy; p. 74*l* Action Plus Sports Images/ Alamy; p. 74*r* SFL Travel/ Alamy; p. 75 Alex Hubenov/ Shutterstock; p. 76 Mario Lopes/ Shutterstock; p. 77*l* Ron Jaffe/ NBCU Photo Bank/NBCUniversal/ Getty Images; p. 77*tr* Angel Fitor/ Science Photo Library; p. 77*br* actionplus sports images/ ActionPlus; p. 78 Kochneva Tetyana/ Shutterstock; p. 79 David Parker/ Science Photo Library; p. 82 JPL/ NASA; p. 88 mycola/iStock/ Thinkstock; p. 93*l* NASA/Bryan Allen/Encyclopedia/ Corbis; p. 93*r* JPL/ NASA; p. 94 / NASA; p. 95*r* David Parker/ Science Photo Library; p. 95*c* NASA/ESA/STSCI/J.-Y. LI (Planetary Science Institute)/ Hubble Comet ISON Imaging Science Team/ Science Photo Library; p. 95*l* Russell Kightley/ Science Photo Library; p. 97 Stocktrek Images, Inc./ Alamy

Cover artwork by Bill Bolton

l = left, *r* = right, *t* = top, *b* = bottom, *c* = centre